HISTORY OF THE St. JAMES HOTEL
CIMARRON, NEW MEXICO

Kevin McDevitt

with Ed Sitzberger

Cimarron Press

Copyright © 2018 Kevin McDevitt

First printing 2019

ISBN: 978-0-9994979-0-6

Library of Congress Control Number: 2018908342

Published by Cimarron Press
Colorado Springs, Colorado

Printed in United States

Cover Design by Wyatt McDevitt

For all general information, please contact Cimarron Press:

sales@cimarronpress.com

Visit us on the Internet at www.cimarronpress.com

Also visit us at www.historyofthestjameshotelcimarronnm.com

To the Village of Cimarron and the people of
New Mexico

Table of Contents

THE OLD WEST SALOON – POEM BY FRED LAMBERT VII

ACKNOWLEDGMENTS IX

INTRODUCTION: HISTORY VS. LEGEND XI

AUTHOR'S NOTE XIII

FORWARD XVI

PART 1: HENRI LAMBERT - PROPRIETOR 1

YOUNG HENRI 2

AMERICA AND THE CIVIL WAR 4

HENRY AND PRESIDENT LINCOLN 6

ANNA ELIZABETH STEPP, CIVILIAN LIFE, AND GOING WEST 10

NEW MEXICO 16

THE SALOON AND EARLY LIFE IN CIMARRON 18

MARY ELIZABETH DAVIS AND FAMILY 24

HENRY AND MARY ELIZABETH 32

PART 2: THE ORIGINAL SALOON, BILLIARD PARLOR, AND INN / THE KILLINGS 1872-1884 39

THE ORIGINAL STRUCTURE AND BEGINNING (SANTA FE TRAIL ERA) 40

LAMBERT'S SALOON 45

THE WILD WEST YEARS AND KILLINGS 53

NARRATIVES OF THE GUNFIGHTS AND KILLINGS 56

    Buffalo Soldiers Killed by David "Davy" Crockett and Gus Heffron 56

    Monte Dealer Juan Borrego Killed by David "Davy" Crockett 59

    Ranchero Francisco "Pancho" Griego Killed by Clay Allison 59

    John Black Killed by Clay Allison 62

    Marshal John Wilson Killed by Clay Allison 62

    Gambler Pomeroy Laughlin Killed by Wall Henderson 65

    Juan Benito Archuleta Killed by Henry Lambert 66

    Cattle Rustlers Killed by Sheriff Rinehart 66

    Bill Curren Killed by Bob Ford, Dick Liddil, Chas Walker, or Wall Henderson 66

    Charles Morris Killed by Chunk Colbert 67

    Feliciano Butarus Killed by Sam Tipton 68

    Soldier from Fort Union 6th Cav., Killed by Francisco "Pancho" Griego. Two Others Wounded 69

THE WEST WAS REALLY WILD 71

PART 3: THE ADDITION **72**

HENRY'S GRAND HOTEL 73
NEWSPAPER ACCOUNTS OF CONSTRUCTION 79
INSIDE THE ST. JAMES 82
PICTORIAL HISTORY OF THE HOTEL 86

PART 4: THE GUESTS OF THE ST. JAMES HOTEL **96**

THE REGISTER 97
HENRY'S RECORDS 109
  Credit Sheets 110

PART 5: AFTER HENRY **112**

TIME MOVES ON: THE DON DIEGO HOTEL 113
A NEW BEGINNING FOR THE ST. JAMES HOTEL 117
LIST OF OWNERS TO PRESENT DAY 118

LAST THOUGHTS **119**

EXTRAS **121**

HENRY'S RECIPES 121
  Sherry Pork Tenderloin 121
  Sauce 122
  Pureed Carrots 122
  Roasted Potatoes 123
ADDITIONAL PICTURES 124

BIBLIOGRAPHY & RESOURCES **149**

The Old Frontier Saloon

I'm head'in for Lambert's frontier saloon-

   The old one down at the St. James hotel;

You can travel near or far

   But you won't find such a bar

      As the one they got down thar-

         It's mighty swell.

I'm bettin' you'll surely enjoy it-

   It's got real western atmosphere;

I'm ornery and I'm lanky

   When it comes to drinks, I'm cranky,

      But this old bar is mighty swanky-

         Have a beer!

You oughta see the frontier paintings-

   Where the old Indian fights were fit;

There's ropin' scenes and brandin'

   Why you feel like you was standin'

      By the ol' cook and the chuck-wagon handy-

         Grab your tools, come and git it.

I'm sure you'll like this old timey saloon-

   What you want.....whiskey, beer or gin?

On Saturday night if you want to make life rosy

   Drop in at Lambert's—It's mighty cozy

      You'll find it sure is a "dozy"!

         Drop your reins – come on in.

---- Fred Lambert Circa 1948

Acknowledgments

To my wonderful family for enduring my quest to write this book. For putting up with the countless hours in front of the computer, my traveling across the country to museums, libraries, government buildings, and other locations, along with my endless discussing of the subject for years. I cannot express my love enough!

Thanks to the Lambert family for being so gracious and allowing me to attend the "Lambert Family Reunion" at the St. James Hotel with you! Thanks to Lucille Langeman for guiding me through the Lambert family tree and sharing our love of history. To Arline Louise "Lambert" Linzinski for helping with the family history and assisting me in deciphering the Lambert property deed documents.

A special thank you to Fred (fourth generation descendant of Henry Lambert) and Rosie Lambert for inviting me into your home and making me feel so welcomed. For listening to my theories and research while writing this book. I appreciate your feedback and friendship. You guys are great!

Thanks to the many Librarians, Assistant Librarians, Museum Directors, Curators, County Clerks, and everyone else who put up with my questions and requests.

Thanks to Mr. Bob Funk and the management and staff of the St. James Hotel in Cimarron, New Mexico for all the assistance and allowing me to have access to the hotel and its history.

A very special thanks to Ed and Sandy Sitzberger for putting me up in your lovely home over the years on my many trips to

Cimarron. For our morning conversations over breakfast and adult beverages in the evening. You guys are special. My love and appreciation are enduring. You are my dear friends and I thank you.

To Ed Sitzberger, my cohort on this project. As a former owner of the St. James Hotel and the person responsible for bringing this grand old hotel back to her original glory, I thank you. Your knowledge of the hotel, its history, and construction was invaluable. I cannot express how much I enjoyed walking through the halls of the St. James listening to your stories. You are a dear friend and it was an honor to work with you.

Last, but not least, a heartfelt thanks to Jean Sitzberger, my old friend of so many years who introduced me to her father, Ed, the St. James Hotel, and its history…this is all your fault! You are part of our family forever.

Introduction: History Vs. Legend

In writing this book, one of the main issues was separating history from legend. Over the course of many years, I have written letters, interviewed family members, talked with historical societies, spent countless hours in libraries and archives, read numerous books, and searched the internet to bring the real story of Henry Lambert and the St. James Hotel to light. The first thing I found was that the many books, websites, and articles either mentioning or about Henry and the St. James Hotel were all different in some way or another. So, which ones were true and where did all these conflicting stories come from?

Henry's life was first chronicled in a biographical sketch of prominent New Mexico citizens in the 1891 book, *History of New Mexico-Helen Haines*. Then again in 1907 in *History of New Mexico-Anderson*. Even beloved author and New Mexico historian F. Stanley wrote of Henry's life in his books *The Grant that Maxwell Bought* - 1952, *One Half Mile from Heaven...The Cimarron Story* - 1949, and *The Raton Chronicles* - 1948, but again, with obvious disparities in all these books.

I quickly realized I needed to address this historically and be as unbiased a possible. In looking at all the research I had done and putting data into a timeline program, I quickly realized things were amiss. Henry's life simply did not add up…from a chronological perspective anyway. Great care was taken to concentrate on dates and events to come up with a logical timeline of the endeavors in Henry's life. With today's incredible access to specific historical data (libraries, museums, and historical archives), even compared to ten years ago, an account of Henry's life began to appear.

Looking into military records, Naval salary records from the Civil War, IRS tax assessments (yes, even in the 1860s), marriage records, death records, census records, property deeds, newspaper accounts, and much, much more they began to paint a picture of the milestones in Henry's life…and what a life it was! The good news is we have decent documentable evidence of much of Henry's life; the other side is we will be challenging old legends. Also, new discoveries of Henry's life were found adding even more to the mystique of this incredible man.

What all this research showed is that this man and his hotel were part of a "convergence in time" where one man inadvertently met or came to know so many historical figures of the time period and the Old West. Mace Bowman, Pawnee Bill, Clay Allison, Lucien Maxwell, Kit Carson, John Chisum, Bat and James Masterson, W.F. Cody, Fredrick Remington, and likely Abraham Lincoln and General Ulysses S. Grant…the list goes on. How is it this one hotel came to be the conduit for so many famous, and infamous, Old West characters in history?

So, whether "History or Legend," the wonderful thing about the St. James Hotel is it's like stepping back a century or more in time. Much of the hotel has not changed and it is still as it was in the 1880s. The original saloon, the original addition, and the original bullet holes in the pressed tin ceiling are still there. In the late hours of the night, if you are quiet and if you listen hard, you can hear them. For these characters still walk its halls, drink at its bar, and play poker in the saloon just as they did so many years before.

Author's Note

"A story to be told"

In the early 1990s, I had the privilege of becoming friends with Jean Sitzberger, as we both worked for the same company in Albuquerque. Jean quickly learned of my passion for Old West history. After learning of this, Jean told me, "You need to meet my father. He owns the St. James Hotel in Cimarron, New Mexico."

"When can we go?!" I replied. Well, shortly afterward I made my first trip of many to Cimarron where I met Jean's father, Ed Sitzberger, and his wife, Sandy. Ed, Sandy, and I also became good friends. Ed was very patient as I quizzed him about every aspect of the hotel. I carefully listened and took in all the stories and history of the St. James. Ed walked through the hotel giving me an incredible hands-on history lesson showing me rooms and even allowing me to scroll through the old guest registry.

Needless to say, Ed and I now had one thing in common…a love for the St. James Hotel. My wife and I made many trips back to Cimarron and always stayed with Ed and Sandy in their home behind the St. James Hotel, which is also the old National Hotel on the Santa Fe Trail that has been converted into a family residence. Sometime in the mid-1990s over lunch, Ed asked if I would do him a favor. He told me he had heard that Fred Lambert, who is the son of the original hotel owner, left behind a diary and he wanted to know if I would look for it. He said it might be at the University of New Mexico in Albuquerque. This simple request would have a profound impact on my life.

After getting home, I called the University library and asked if they had any material from Fred Lambert of Cimarron, New Mexico. After being connected to the Center for Southwest Research on campus, I asked the question again and, to my surprise, the young lady said they had a box containing possessions of his. I asked if it contained a diary or journal and their reply was that they did not know what was in the box. Of course, I immediately asked if I could come and look through it. They very graciously granted my request and would have it available the next day.

Jean, my wife, and I went down to the Center for Southwest Research to find a small box waiting for us. As we opened it, we saw it was full of papers and a couple of books. We started the task of sifting through the papers which consisted of personal writings, notes, western poetry (which Fred Lambert wrote, I found out), sketches, and diagrams. Unfortunately, there was no diary or journal. The staff assisted me in making copies of as much as we could and packed up the box.

Once home, I started to read through the writings and came to a couple of conclusions. First, Fred Lambert was quite the poet and artist. Second, he had taken the time to write down and collect a lot of history of the St. James Hotel. He had copied the names out of the original guest registry and put them in alphabetical order. He even went as far as sketching out detailed drawings of where people had been shot and killed within the hotel. There were also numerous hand-written notes on the history of the hotel. These were events and stories he had heard, been told, or seen in his lifetime...and this gentleman had seen quite a bit! Remember, we are talking about someone whose godfather is said to be Buffalo Bill Cody and whose own father knew Lucien Maxwell, Clay Allison, Francisco "Pancho" Griego, David "Davy" Crockett, and Wyatt Earp.

I quickly realized that he had a love for the St. James Hotel and what I gathered from reading his notes was a regret that the hotel had slipped out of the family's control. The point here is that he went to a lot of trouble to do all these things…but for what reason? Personally, I think he intended to tell the history of the St. James Hotel and his father, but through life's many twists and turns, along with a very abrupt death, never had the chance to complete the project. Fred Lambert not only had a love for the St. James, but a passion for New Mexico, and his beloved Cimarron. These affections are very evident in his poetry, his writings, and his art.

Over the years, I have gone back to these notes from the box in the library, as well as Fred's writings many times and have concluded that this is a story Fred wanted to be told. Why else would he go to all the trouble to write this down and collect all this information? I think it would be a shame to let this story die in a box on a library shelf. The St. James Hotel and Henry Lambert, its original owner, is a story waiting to be told and is a wonderful piece of New Mexico history. This is a story of the founding family, the hotel, and its guests.

Kevin McDevitt

Author/Historian

Forward

Of the thousands of photos I've taken in New Mexico, the eighth was of the St. James Hotel. It was November 2005 and I'd never been to Cimarron before, but I was instantly drawn to the regal old hostelry. In fact, the St. James turned out to be the *only* place I would photograph in Cimarron until I returned almost six years later, this time to spend the night. I stayed in Mary's Room, #17, reportedly haunted by the ghost of Henry Lambert's first wife. While I didn't detect the smell of roses, the tell-tale sign of Mary's presence, I did find the creaking and groaning of the wooden hallway floor strangely comforting. Across that hallway was #18, which you couldn't stay in due to the violence of its resident spirits, although they might be temporarily tamed by an offering of whiskey. There were still bullet holes in the tin ceiling of the saloon. Bat Masterson stayed here. So, did Kit Carson. Jesse James and his killer, Bob Ford. Wyatt Earp, too. Clay Allison shot an untold number of people both inside and out. Can it all be true? Does it even matter?!

Well, to anyone that cares about history and wishes to have a reasonable understanding of the present, the answer to that last question is an emphatic, "Yes, it absolutely matters!" And this is where Kevin McDevitt and his friend Ed Sitzberger, owner of the St. James from 1985 to 1993, have done us all a great service. To write *History of the St. James Hotel* old newspapers were combed through and cross-referenced, diaries and personal documents read and re-read, numerous interviews conducted, and the St. James itself given the once-over twice. Or maybe three times. All of this work shows in the myths debunked or set aside as "evidence inconclusive," but even more important is the truth that emerges in the shape of Henry Lambert, his family, his friends, and his wonderful Wild West hotel, which indeed saw the frontier blossom.

History of the St. James Hotel is an important addition to the historical literature of New Mexico and aficionados of western history will find much to add to their own understanding of the Old West and its cast of characters. In fact, the only thing that might be better than reading this book is staying in the St. James itself. And, should you decide to read *History of the St. James Hotel* before bedtime in room #17, Mary might well fill the air with the fragrance of roses in a show of appreciation for how Kevin and Ed have brought the oft-clouded story of the Lambert family and their hotel into the light with the utmost care and respect.

So, check your gun at the bar and ask to be dealt in for the next round. Oh, and remember not to sit with your back to the door. This is still the St. James, after all.

John Mulhouse – City of Dust

Albuquerque, NM

History of the St. James Hotel
Cimarron, New Mexico

Part 1: Henri Lambert - Proprietor

Henri Lambert at 16 years of age. (Courtesy Lambert Family)

Young Henri

Henri Lambert was born on Sunday, October 28, in the year 1838 in Nantes, Loire-Atlantique, Pays de la Loire, France to Ro and Mary Lambert. Henri's parents planned for him to study the priesthood, but Henri, who dreamed of a life of adventure and girls, had different ideas and ran away from home around the age of 12. Henri was quickly found by his parents and sent to learn the art of cooking in Le Havre, France. At about the age of 14, he was sent to work at his uncle's hotel. This is where Henri would learn the hotel and cooking trades.

At approximately age 18 and yearning for adventure, he ships out on a vessel bound for South America. He eventually leaves the service of the ship in Montevideo, Peru. From there Henri journeys to Buenos Aires, joining a circus troupe traveling from port to port as the cook. He eventually goes back to sea and travels more of the world. Multiple stories have Henri traveling to South America, Cuba, England, and the east coast of the United States. He returns to Le Havre, France roughly in the years 1858-59.

Around this time, Henri joins and serves in the Papal Army for Pope Pius IX. He is part of the Papal Zouaves [zoo-ahv], which is a private army created to defend the southern Papal states of Italy. These southern Italian states are owned by the Catholic Church and the Pope during this era. Italian nationalists wishing to reunite Italy begin a revolution against the Pope. It is unknown if Henri is sent to fight for the Pope by his parents or if he joined himself. Henri is seen here in the very distinct uniform of a Papal Zouaves soldier. He is around 20 or 21 years old in this picture and would stand 5 feet 7 inches tall. Sometime after leaving the service of the Papal Zouaves, he returns home to France and plans to head for America.

Henri Lambert at about 20-21 years of age in his Papal Zouaves uniform. (Courtesy Lambert Family)

America and the Civil War

In 1861, Henri embarks for America on a French sailing vessel and arrives in Philadelphia later that year. He meets up with Frenchman Brutus de Villerio who will design the first submarine for the U.S. Navy. Henri becomes part of the civilian crew who all speak French. He is listed as an Assistant Engineer. In a contract book of the Bureau of Yards and Docks (National Archives), an agreement on November 1, 1861 states: "Henri Lambert to serve as an 'operative' in the submarine 'Propeller' at the rate of $24.00 per month and $16.00 per month for substance and necessary clothing and further agree to sign an oath of allegiance to the United States. The Navy Department agrees to pay monthly wages, with $10.00 bounty each on signing this agreement, as bounty for engaging in perilous services of the Propeller."

The submarine later changes its name to the "Alligator" and the civilian crew is replaced with a U.S. Union Navy crew and is officially recognized as the U.S. Navy's first submarine. The Alligator sinks off the coast of Cape Hatteras, South Carolina in 1863 while being towed to a mission in Charleston Harbor and has yet to be found. Henri leaves service of the Propeller on May 1, 1862, as the Navy takes over the submarine and signs on board a sailing ship to Europe. He returns to America after three months. On October 6, 1862, he joins the Union Navy serving three years as a Captain's Steward. This is during the time of the Civil War.

Note: sometime in the mid-1860s we start to see documents where Henri is changing the spelling of his name from Henri to Henry, using the American vernacular from that point on.

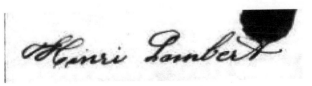

In mid-1864, he settles in the City Point/Petersburg, Virginia area. This is likely because he was stationed at the port of Norfolk, Virginia when his enlistment in the Union Navy ended. It is also rumored that Henry was released from the Navy early because of a shipboard accident. Another story, mentioned in a couple of documents, states Henry deserted from the Navy a few months after joining. This is highly unlikely for several reasons. One is Henry's character. This type of action just doesn't fit as he was not known to back down from a challenge. Another is between 1862 and 1864 no documentation of Henry's whereabouts could be found. This would be consistent with him being on a ship. One of these sources states that after deserting Henry joined the Army as a cook. Remember in those days, desertion was a very serious offense punishable by death, physical punishment, or prison time. It is unlikely anyone would desert one service, then join another for fear of being found out. Lastly, later in life Henry joined the Grand Army of the Republic, or GAR, a fraternal organization of Civil War military service veterans. Would he do this if he was a deserter?

IRS records show Henry being in the port of Norfolk or Petersburg, Virginia area in August/September 1864 as a "retail dealer of liquor" owing $6.67 in taxes. In 1865-66, IRS records show Henry in the City Point, Virginia area running an eating house. City Point, Virginia was at this time occupied by the Union Army for the "Siege of Petersburg" against southern forces. It was also the largest port in the world during this time of the Civil War and likewise headquarters for General Ulysses S. Grant.

Henry and President Lincoln

In previous articles and writings, it has been stated that Henry Lambert was a cook in the fifth Union Army Corps for General Warren and General Grant. It has also been stated that Henry was a chef or even possibly head chef at the White House for President Lincoln. Two books on the history of New Mexico (*Haines 1891 & Anderson 1907*) have biographical sections on prominent citizens of New Mexico. Both of these books include a section on Henry and Mary Elizabeth Lambert, Henry's second wife, but neither mentioned Henry being a chef for President Lincoln. It should be noted both books were written while Henry was alive, and he was most likely consulted about his life for each of the books. One book states he was a personal cook for General Grant, the other a cook for General Warren, but neither state he was a cook for the president. Again, it's amazing that no two stories told about Henry are the same.

After contacting the White House Historical Association, talking with President Lincoln and Mary Lincoln scholars, and conducting an exhaustive search, there is no evidence of Henry ever being a cook or chef at the White House. This includes White House payroll records from that time. It should also be noted that there is no mention of Henry being a personal cook or chef in Ulysses S. Grant's memoirs published in 1885. The first written account of Henry being a chef at the White House was in the 1952 book *Satan's Paradise* written by Agnes Morley Cleaveland some 39 years after Henry's death. Henry's son, Fred Lambert, was a contributor to the book.

The only possible physical evidence we might have had is a print of President Lincoln and his family. According to Henry's son, Fred Lambert, in a 1957 Albuquerque Journal newspaper article, the print was given to his father by Lincoln after he left the White House and was Fred's prized possession. The back of the wooden print frame houses a written note which reads: "This picture given to Henry Lambert by President Lincoln on Lambert's departure from the White House March 1863." The issue here is that this notation is in Fred Lambert's handwriting, not President Lincoln's or Henry Lambert's.

After Lincoln's death, there was a mania from all over the world for Lincoln memorabilia. Unscrupulous companies would copy legitimate Lincoln pictures, etchings, or paintings on a large scale. Then sell these on the black market by the hundreds of thousands. Unfortunately, this appears to be a low-quality copy of a copy that was produced in late 1865 following Lincoln's death in April of that same year.

The Philadelphia Print Shop, where you can still buy this print, lists it as ["F. Schell. "Lincoln Family." Philadelphia: John Dainty, [ca. 1865 ff.]. Steel engraving by A.B. Walter. 8 1/4 x 6 (oval image) plus margins. Although not giving proper credit, this picture is inspired by Matthew Brady's famous portrait of President Lincoln reading to Tad on February 4, 1864. Added to the print is Mary Todd Lincoln and son Robert behind the president who is reading a Bible. We can assume it is a Bible because the clasps on the back cover represent a typical housing for the times. A portrait of the son, Willie, who died in the White House is on the far wall."]

Fred Lambert's copy of this print is currently in the Old Aztec Mill Museum that was built by Lucien Maxwell in 1864 in Cimarron, New Mexico, which contains much of Cimarron's history and is well worth visiting.

Lambert copy of the Lincoln print (front)

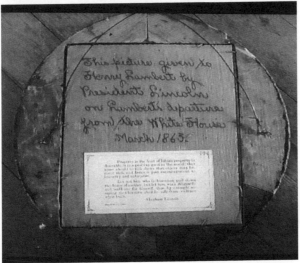

Fred Lambert's handwriting on the back (Both pictures Courtesy of Jerry Hoover)

Possible Scenario

But alas, there may be a few scenarios that could explain versions of the story. At a time in 1864-65 all four men, General Warren, General Grant, President Lincoln, and Henry Lambert, were all in the City Point, Virginia area during the Civil War. It is conceivable these men somehow interacted during that time. Henry could have been contracted to cook at General Grant's headquarters at City Point where President Lincoln visited multiple times. Also, he could have possibly met all these men as he was running an eating house in the area during these years.

Another scenario is Henry, who was still serving in the Union Navy as a steward, was aboard the *U.S.S. Baltimore* which the President traveled on during his visits to see Grant at City Point, Virginia from Washington, D.C. in June of 1864.

It is the author's belief that Henry did cook for President Lincoln and Generals Grant and Warren in some capacity, just not at the White House. We will continue to wait for documentable evidence to shed more light on these events.

Anna Elizabeth Stepp, Civilian Life, and Going West

From IRS statements of mid-1864 through 1866 Henry is selling commercial goods and running an eating house in the City Point/Petersburg, Virginia area. This is where he meets his first wife, Anna Elizabeth Stepp. Anna was born in 1846 in Halifax County, Virginia. Anna Elizabeth Stepp and Henry Lambert were married on March 28, 1868. She was 22. They were married in Petersburg, Dinwiddie County, Virginia.

Anna liked going by nicknames; she used Mollie the most. During her married life, she would go by Mollie or Mary Lambert. Except for the 1880 census record, the name Mollie Lambert appears on all written documentation. This would include, but is not limited to, the 1870 census record, all of her and Henry's official documents, and the mention of her death in the newspaper. Curiously enough, one of the few places the name Mary Lambert is written is on her headstone.

Mary (Stepp) Lambert was considered a very strong woman for her day and insisted on being named on many of the legal documents along with Henry. She also had business dealings in the Cimarron area on her own.

In 1868, Henry gets gold fever and sells his restaurant at auction. He contracts with an auction company who advertises in the Petersburg Progress newspaper March 26, 1868.

AUCTION SALE OF BAR-ROOM FIXTURES, LIQUORS, &c.—Messrs. Davenport, Fitlz & Davis will commence the sale this day at 10 o'clock, of the bar-room and bakery fixtures, and all the stock in the house occupied by Henry Lambert, No 3 Old Market Square. We understand that there is quite a large stock on hand, and as it is all to be closed out to-day, bargains may be obtained.

Henry heads west to the gold boom on Baldy Mountain, outside of Elizabethtown, New Mexico. He takes Mary, her mother Nancy, who is widowed, and brothers Nathan, Bob (Robert), and Willie west as far as Clay County, Missouri to stay with some of their relatives. He would send for them once he was established out west. Henry makes his way to Westport Landing Kansas City, Missouri, near Independence.

Henry's first wife, Anna Elizabeth Stepp, at 16 years of age (Courtesy Lambert Family)

Westport Landing was a terminus for the Santa Fe Trail and a very large river port transporting supplies westward.

From here it is unclear exactly how Henry got out west. One story goes that Henry went to Denver by train and another tells of him going west by stage line. Both modes of transportation were active during this time period. The intercontinental railroad would be completed in the coming year of 1869 and stage lines were still actively running.

Hockaday and Hall Stage Line published this advertisement in the *Western Journal of Commerce* in Kansas City, and it will give the reader an inside glimpse of what it was to travel by stage in this era:

The United States mail from independence to Santa
FE, New Mexico - SEMI - MONTHLY

Santa Fe traders and those desirous of crossing the plains to New Mexico are informed that the undersigned will carry the U.S. mail from Independence to Santa Fe for four years, commencing on the first day of July 1857, in stages drawn by six mules.

The stage is to leave Independence and Santa Fe on the first and 15ᵗʰ of each month. They will be entirely new and comfortable for passengers; well-guarded, and running through each way in from 20 to 25 days. Travelers to and from New Mexico will doubtless find this the safest and most expeditious and comparable, as well as the cheapest mode of crossing the plains.

FARE THROUGH

From November 1st to May 1st..........$150.00

From May 1st to November 1st..........$125.00

Provisions, all arms, and ammunition furnished by the proprietors.

Packages and extra baggage will be transported, when possible to do so, at the rate of 35¢ per pound in summer, and 50¢ per pound in winter, but no packages will be charged less than $1.00.

The proprietors will not be responsible for any package worth more than $50.00 unless contents given and specially contracted for, and all baggage at all times at the risk of the owner thereof.

In all cases the passenger money must be paid in advance, and passengers must stipulate to conform to the rules which may be established by the undersigned, for the government of their line of stages, and those traveling with them on the plains.

No passenger allowed more than 40 pounds of baggage in addition to the necessary bedding.

Mr. Levi Speidleburg, at Santa Fe, and J. & W.R. Bernard & Co., at Westport, Mo., and our conductor and agents are authorized to engage passengers and receipts for passage Monday.

Hockaday & Hall

One of Fred Lambert's favorite stories was about his father's trip out west to New Mexico. Again, not knowing how Henry got out west, it is not clear if the story is factual or slightly embellished...either way, it's a great story!

The story goes...After booking a trip on a stage line, Henry soon realized he was the only passenger. After inquiring to the stage driver, he explained that Indian attacks had slowed business greatly. The only other person on the stage besides Henry and the driver was the guard riding shotgun. Since there were only the three of them on the stage, everyone took a turn helping out. Henry had no idea how to handle horses or drive the stagecoach, so he helped out by riding shotgun to give the others a chance to sleep in the stage. Somewhere outside of McPherson, Kansas, Henry was riding shotgun and spotted smoke in the distance. Henry pointed the smoke out to the driver, who yelled "Indians!"

The driver turned the rig toward McPherson, trying to outrun the Indians who had already spotted the stage. It was not long until the driver realized they were gaining on the stage quickly. The driver decided to stop the stage and grab the mailbag, unhook the mules and ride them into town as quickly as possible. This was Henry's first time on a mule, and he was riding for his life. Henry was bouncing all over the mule and hanging onto the collar with all his might.

Henry and the stagehands rode into McPherson in a cloud of dust. They made quite an entrance and gathered a crowd quickly. A group of armed men organized and rode out to the prairie. By the time the men got to where the stage was abandoned, it had been set on fire and burned to the ground. Nothing was left and all of Henry's belongings were destroyed. Luckily, Henry kept all of his money on him, but his trip had come to a sudden halt.

Henry wandered around McPherson for a couple of days contemplating what he was going to do. He eventually caught wind of a wagon train heading west for Fort Union, New Mexico and joined on as the cook. During Henry's time with the wagon train, he tried his hand at buffalo hunting. However, he very quickly found out that he enjoyed staying in camp and cooking much more than hunting.

One day as the wagon train was resting on the prairie a group of men came riding into camp. This is where Henry met the famed frontiersman Kit Carson. Kit, like everyone else in camp, was very impressed with Henry's cooking and said he would put in a good word for him with Lucien Maxwell of Maxwell Land Grant fame. Carson and Maxwell were good friends from their time together as scouts. Carson and Maxwell both lived in Rayado, New Mexico before Maxwell moved his rancho to Cimarron.

The two groups say their farewells and Henry continues with the wagon train as it slowly makes its way toward the Rocky Mountains. As the wagon train enters the high country, Henry abandons it for a faster mode of transportation and books passage on a stagecoach. He travels on to Maxwell's rancho in the town of Cimarron where he meets the great land baron, Lucien B. Maxwell, owner of almost two million acres of a Mexican Land Grant.

New Mexico

Maxwell had heard of Henry from Kit Carson "as the story goes" and asks him to stay on as a cook at his mansion, but Henry decides to head west some 45 miles to Elizabethtown, New Mexico to make his fortune. New Mexico's first incorporated town, Elizabethtown, also known as E-Town, was a booming gold mining camp in the area of Mount Baldy. Henry begins panning for gold in the Moreno Valley near Virginia City, an area of the Maxwell Land Grant named after Maxwell's daughter. After trying his luck at placer mining Henry realizes there were other ways to make gold. So, he started a business to serve the miners, most likely a restaurant. Henry pays $6.50 in personal taxes according to the "Record of Taxes in the Collection District of New Mexico" in 1868.

In the Mora deed book on May 20, 1868, Henry buys the "north one half of the house situated on Lot No. (1) one, in Block No. (11) Eleven, together with the front of ground on which it stands in the town of Elizabethtown" for the sum of $1,700.00 from Lewis Mace. He also goes on to buy property with improvements in Elizabethtown at auction on December 28, 1868, consisting of a small log framed hotel and restaurant fronting Second Street. The hotel was named the "E-Town Hotel," one of two hotels in town. Mora County deeds say: "Lot No. Y, in block No. 3, fronting second street 50 feet and back 40 feet." Henry sends for Mary and family and they arrive sometime in early 1869. The 1870 census records show Henry, at 31 years of age, and Mary Lambert as hotel owners in Elizabethtown, New Mexico, their property holdings worth $5,000. Mary's brother, Nathan Stepp, was also living with them at that time. Henry is now a permanent resident of New Mexico. Things were starting well for the Lamberts.

In 1871, Henry recognizes the possibilities of the up and coming town of Cimarron, New Mexico and its election to the latest county seat of the newly organized Colfax County. At this time, two stories emerge. One tells of Henry selling his holdings in E-Town and moving to Cimarron; the other of him leasing his E-Town hotel to a man named Farrand and moving to Cimarron, then finally liquidating his E-Town holding in 1875 for a tidy profit. Either way, Henry was turning into a shrewd businessman. During this period many things were changing, and Cimarron was transitioning from a life centered around Lucien Maxwell's rancho. In 1870, Maxwell sold his land grant to a group of English and Dutch speculators that formed the Maxwell Land Grant and Railway Company (MLG&RC). Maxwell moved to Fort Sumner, New Mexico where he lived until his death in 1875. On a historical note, Billy the Kid was shot by Pat Garrett in Maxwell's Fort Sumner home in 1881, then owned by his son, Pete.

The Saloon and Early Life in Cimarron

One of the continuing questions about Henry after moving to Cimarron in 1871: Does he purchase the saloon? After a thorough search of county records, two deeds were found of Henry buying a portion of the Maxwell House along with the saloon and hotel in 1875. But they also state Henry was occupying these properties beforehand. Another source (*History of New Mexico-Anderson*) states in the fall of 1871 Henry "purchased a place from Grant." This awkwardly stated phrase implies that Henry bought the saloon from the Maxwell Land Grant and Railway Company, the new owners of the Maxwell Land Grant, in 1871. Newspaper accounts also show that Henry becomes proprietor and opens the saloon and inn, or small boarding house, in 1871-72. The biggest piece of evidence we have is a customer credit sheet of Henry's from the saloon and inn with the date December of 1871. This shows Henry was definitively operating the saloon and inn at this time. This credit sheet is shown later in the book under "Henry's Records." More detail on this in Parts 2 and 3.

In early 1876 Henry and Mary adopted a son, Jacob "Jake" Vantular. The 1880 census records show Jacob at 5 years old and he is listed as Henry and Mary's adopted son. The exact adoption dates are unclear. Not much is known about Jacob during his childhood or his time in Cimarron. Later in life, Jacob was a mining laborer in the State of Oklahoma per 1920 census records. He was also married to Dora A. Sivers in Webb City, Missouri, October 17, 1919. Jacob passed sometime before 1940 in Oklahoma, as Dora is listed as a widow in the 1940 census.

On November 17, 1879, Henry enters an agreement to purchase the remainder of the block and lots around the St. James Hotel for an addition. The original saloon would be the structure that was incorporated into the new hotel addition. This old section

Jacob "Jake" Vantuler, adopted son of Henry and Anna Stepp Lambert.

(Courtesy Lambert Family)

is the current dining room area, bar, and lobby. Henry enters into the agreement with Frank R. Sherwin (Manager of the Maxwell Land Grant & Railway Company) "for block A.S.W, lots; 1, 2, 3, 4, and all buildings thereon, paid $2,250.00 at 7% interest to be paid in 10 years, with exception to make improvement to build a large and commodious hotel as it is to be hereafter and to spend not less than $4000 in construction."

In 1880, at the age of 41, Henry begins construction on a 25-room expansion that will become the historical St. James Hotel. All the local newspapers reported updates on the status of construction. The Raton Guard newspaper in a December 1881 issue reported: "Lambert incorporated the original bar and billiard parlor into the edifice, thus preserving for future generations the room that saw the frontier blossom." More detail on the hotel addition in part 3.

In 1881, Henry's wife, Mary (Stepp), contracts an illness. It is unclear what the illness was, although consumption or pneumonia are most likely, but it lasted through the year. Mary's illness peaked in October of 1881 with the construction of the hotel addition almost complete. The Lamberts were living in the completed east wing of the hotel at the time. Mary passes away on October 28, 1881, in Cimarron, New Mexico in the St. James Hotel on her husband's 43rd birthday. She was never able to enjoy the grand opening of the St. James Hotel as planned. Mary passed away at the age of 35 and was buried in Mountain View Cemetery in Cimarron, New Mexico next to her brother, Willie, who had died the previous month. Henry wore black for an entire year in memory of Mary. Henry and Mary were married for 13 years. On her headstone it is inscribed:

To the memory of
MARY
WIFE OF
HENRY LAMBERT
DIED AT
Cimarron, N.M.
October 28, 1881
AGED
35 Years
'Deeply regretted by all
who knew her'

Headstone of Mary (Stepp) Lambert, Henry's first wife
(Author's collection)

Left to Right: William "Willie" Stepp at age 16. Nancy Stepp, mother of Mary (Stepp) Lambert and Willie Stepp. (Courtesy Lambert Family)

On a sad note, Mary's mother, Nancy Stepp, and her brother, William "Willie" Stepp, had moved to Cimarron years earlier. In the month of September 1881, Nancy Stepp lost three of her children. Willie on September 1st in Cimarron (Chief Justice L. Bradford Prince who would become Territorial Governor of New Mexico rendered services as there were no clergy in Cimarron in those years), Nathan B. "Dock" Stepp on September 6th in Missouri, Edward Stepp on September 9th (train accident) in Missouri, and then her daughter Anna Elizabeth Stepp (Mary Lambert) on October 28th. Nancy lost four of her ten children in a 60-day time frame in 1881. Nancy left Cimarron and moved to Springer, New Mexico soon afterward.

The new hotel opened on December 1, 1881. It must have been a gala affair, but very much saddened by the loss of Mary. The Raton Guard newspaper in a December 1881 issue reported: "Built at the cost of $17,000 and is one of the finest hotels in the territory." Many notables attended the grand opening of the St. James, including brothers Charles and Frank Springer, Judge W.D. Lee, Henry M. Porter (a prominent merchant in Springer, New Mexico), Don Ramon Abreu, Frank R. Sherwin, the manager of the Maxwell Land Grant and Railway Company, and many others. Over the next 20 years, many famous western figures would stay at the St. James Hotel.

Mary Elizabeth Davis and Family

It was important to Henry to have a wife at his new hotel to give it respectability and get away from its reputation of violence. Henry confided in his brother-in-law Bob Stepp, Mary (Stepp) Lambert's brother, who owned a bar in Cimarron about finding a new wife. Bob said he knew of a man that had five unmarried daughters in Excelsior Springs, Missouri. Soon afterward in 1882, Bob and Henry headed to Springer, New Mexico and caught the passenger train to Missouri. Henry was introduced to the Davis family and Mary Elizabeth Davis took a shining to Henry immediately, but unfortunately, her father did not. He did not like that Henry was a foreigner or the thought of his daughter moving to Cimarron which had been nicknamed "Satan's Paradise." After much pleading by Bob on Henry's behalf and the fact that Mary Elizabeth had not eaten for two days, he relented and allowed his daughter to marry Henry. They were married in Missouri on November 19, 1882, by Minister of the Gospel John P. Bryan (Missouri Marriage Records 1805-2002). Henry and Mary Elizabeth had five sons.

Note: Mary Elizabeth's father eventually cooled down. He and his wife did come to Cimarron and visit their two daughters, Mary Elizabeth and Catherine. The latter married blacksmith A.C. Hoover and moved to Cimarron as well. Henry and A.C. became good friends and A.C. set up his business just down the street from the hotel. The Hoovers are buried next to the Lamberts.

Henry and Mary Elizabeth Davis on their wedding day – 1882 (Courtesy Lambert Family)

Lambert family in the dining room of the St. James Hotel. Left to Right: Mary Elizabeth, Gene, Fred, Frank, William, and Henry Lambert. (Courtesy Lambert Family)

William Henry Lambert was the first son, born September 16, 1883. He was named after little Willie Stepp and his own father, but everyone called him Bill. He would become a cook like his father to make a living but spent time as a cowhand on his father's ranch in Ute Park, New Mexico. Bill acted as manager of the hotel after Henry's passing but would eventually move to California. Bill was wed to Lucy Rebecca Dalton and had nine children. He died February 8, 1953, in California.

William Henry Lambert (Courtesy Lambert Family)

Frank Davis Lambert, the second son, was born on April 1, 1885. He was named after the family attorney, Frank Springer, who was also the attorney for the Maxwell Land Grant and Railway Company, as well as for Mary Elizabeth's side of the family (Davis). Frank would become a carpenter by trade. He married twice; first to Ada Evelyn MacDonald, then to Thelma Viola Hughbanks. Frank had a daughter with each. He was the first to move away from Cimarron, initially to Oregon then to California. Frank died on April 2, 1952, in California.

Frank Davis Lambert (Courtesy Lambert Family)

Charles Fredrick "Fred" Lambert, the third son, was born January 23, 1887. Of all the children, Fred was the most famous. Fred attended the New Mexico Military Institute (NMMI) in Roswell, New Mexico. He would become a poet, author, artist, historian, and a legendary lawman in the Cimarron area and state of New Mexico. Fred would wear badges for multiple law enforcement agencies including the New Mexico Mounted Police, Town Marshal of Cimarron, Colfax County Deputy, Deputy Special Officer for the U.S. Indian Service, New Mexico Cattle Inspector, New Mexico Deputy Game Warden and more. He married Katherine "Katie" Hoover in La Junta, Colorado.

Fred died suddenly February 3, 1971, at a hospital in Raton, New Mexico. At the time of his passing, Fred was working as curator of the Old Aztec Mill Museum in Cimarron. He is buried in Mountain View Cemetery in Cimarron, New Mexico next to his father, Henry, his mother, Mary Elizabeth, and his beloved wife, Katie.

Charles "Fred" Lambert (Courtesy Lambert Family)

Johnnie Lambert, the fourth son, was born August 17, 1889, and died two and a half years later on February 23, 1892. Johnnie's cause of death is unknown, but one story claims that he died by accident in the hotel. Henry took the loss of Johnnie very hard and carried it with him for years. Johnnie is buried in Mountain View Cemetery in Cimarron, New Mexico next to his mother and father.

Johnnie Lambert (Courtesy Lambert Family)

Eugene "Gene" Twitty Lambert, the fifth son, was born April 10, 1893. He was named after a local politician who was a friend of the Lamberts. Gene was a student at the New Mexico Military Institute (NMMI) in Roswell, New Mexico. It is there he met Dessie Evelyn Henning whom he married and together they would have three children. Gene also worked on the family ranch with all his brothers. Gene retired from his railroad job after 40 years and lived in Huntington Park, California until his death on December 27, 1975. Gene was the last of the brothers to pass.

Eugene Twitty Lambert (Courtesy Lambert Family)

Henry and Mary Elizabeth

Henry and Mary Elizabeth had a good life operating the St. James Hotel for many years. They reared a family and were a part of the community. Mary Elizabeth was quite involved in the goings-on of Cimarron. She organized both the First Protestant Community Church in Cimarron and a school, as well as becoming a leader in the area. Local newspaper accounts mention Henry and Mary Elizabeth regularly.

Henry enters a "Homestead Notice" in the Colfax County deed book for a homestead under the United States Homestead Act for 160 acres in 1871 in the Moreno River precinct. This most likely is the start of his 640-acre ranch in Ute Park, New Mexico, about 12 miles west of Cimarron, which supplied much of the beef and other food for the St. James Hotel. In 1885, Henry leased another 640 acres from the Maxwell Land Grant and Railway Company for cattle and horses.

In 1889, Sam Ketchum was captured on the Lambert ranch. Sam was part of the "Black Jack Ketchum Gang" along with his brother, Jack. They had robbed a train near Folsom and had a shoot-out with lawmen in Turkey Creek Canyon, north of Cimarron. Sam was wounded and made his way to the Lambert ranch where he was captured.

The Lamberts owned 20 acres west of the St. James where Mary Elizabeth had a very large garden. This is where she grew vegetables for the hotel and her family. There are several turn of the century plot maps of Cimarron in the Old Aztec Mill Museum showing the Lamberts property and other notable landmarks of the area.

Mary Elizabeth in her garden, near the St. James Hotel. (Courtesy Lambert Family)

Henry registered the "MHL" brand for his cattle and the "ML" brand on the left hip for his horses according to the "Live Stock Journal of New Mexico" section of the July 7, 1887, issue of the Raton Comet.

Henry's brand as registered in the Live Stock Journal of New Mexico

Henry was involved in numerous business ventures and the Colfax County Tax Journal lists charges made to Henry for running the saloon, mercantile store, grocery, a butchery, a feed store, and a stable all in addition to his hotel. Henry maintained fine buggy teams, so visitors to the hotel could go up into the mountains on day trips.

In the Las Vegas Gazette on February 19, 1876, it states: "United States District Court (Santa Fe) for the 1st Judicial District of New Mexico, Hon. Henry L. Walde, Chief Justice, presiding." Henry was on trial (601, U.S. vs. Henry Lambert) for operating as a wholesale liquor dealer. Henry was tried, and the verdict was "not guilty" (602, U.S. vs. Henry Lambert). Henry had also been fined by the New Mexico Territorial Courts for permitting gambling in his establishment.

Apparently, Henry was also an avid collector. In a 1907 article in the Cimarron News and Press newspaper, it stated: "The writer on Thursday last had the pleasure of examining one of the finest collections of curios in the territory of New Mexico, consisting of Indian baskets, arrows, beaded garments formerly worn by the chiefs of the Pueblo Indians, Mexican pottery, old historic firearms, and several fine collections of old coins. These curios are the property of Henry Lambert, proprietor of the St. James Hotel of this city."

Henry studied for his citizenship with Frank Springer, a famous New Mexico land grant attorney and co-founder of the CS ranch. He received his U.S. citizen naturalization on March 13, 1888, through the New Mexico Territory courts and was officially an American citizen. Henry also served the community and was elected as School Director in 1890.

At one time, Henry belonged to the Grand Army of the Republic organization, also known as the GAR. This was a fraternal society for veterans of the Civil War serving in the Union Army, Navy, or Marines. Every state had a GAR Post after the Civil War. There was possibly one in Cimarron or nearby.

Grand Army of the Republic (GAR) Medal issued by the fraternal organization.

In June of 1912, Henry contracts an illness. This, combined with arthritis, sets in motion Henry's passing. In latter days Henry could only walk using a cane. On January 24, 1913, Henry Lambert passes away at 7 p.m. in the St. James Hotel at the age of 75. Thus, ending an era where one man was able to witness Wild West history firsthand, meet legends and notables within western lore and close out the bygone days of the Old West.

Henry Lambert's funeral took place on January 26, 1913, and was the largest funeral held at the time in that part of New Mexico. Henry, the chef from France, who cooked for some of the most notable figures in Western history and his time, who was an adventurer, Civil War soldier, miner, businessman, husband, and father, was buried in Mountain View Cemetery in Cimarron, New Mexico. A large piece of the Old West was buried with him.

Mary Elizabeth Lambert lived until December 8, 1926. She passed away in California while visiting her son, Gene. Mary Elizabeth is buried next to her husband, Henry, in Mountain View Cemetery in Cimarron, New Mexico. Buried in the Lambert plot next to Henry and Mary Elizabeth is their son Johnnie and their grandchild, "Baby Lambert," (died stillborn) child of William Henry Lambert, Henry's first son, and his wife, Luci Rebecka Dalton. Just outside their plot lie their son, Charles Fredrick Lambert, and his wife, Katie. Also, Mary Elizabeth's sister, Catherine, and her husband, A.C. Hoover.

Henry Lambert later in life. In Henry's elder years he used a cane due to arthritis. (Courtesy Arthur Johnson Memorial Library, Raton, New Mexico)

*The headstones of Henry and Mary Elizabeth Lambert in Mountain View
Cemetery, Cimarron, N.M. (Author's collection)*

Part 2: The Original Saloon, Billiard Parlor,

and Inn / The Killings 1872 – 1884

The Original Structure and Beginning (Santa Fe Trail Era)

Cimarron was on the mountain route of the Santa Fe Trail. People tended to take this route instead of the Cimarron Cutoff because there was less of a chance of running into hostiles and a better water supply. You also had Bent's Fort and the Wooten House just before Raton Pass to resupply and rest. The St. Louis, Rocky Mountain & Pacific Railway Company did not get to Cimarron until 1906 when they added a spur from Raton, New Mexico. Until then, everything was shipped into town by wagon. The Santa Fe Trail passed right in front of Lambert's Saloon and Inn going through Cimarron heading south to Fort Union. Henry became famous along the Santa Fe Trail for his cooking of sherry pork tenderloin and Spanish venison. His saloon too became famous, but for different reasons. As time passed, the reputation of Henry's saloon grew. It was a wild place, in wild times…

The original building that housed the saloon and billiard parlor was constructed sometime prior to 1866. This is supported by pictures of the established building standing in the 1866-68 timeframe. The Old Aztec Mill in the following picture was built in 1864 by Lucien Maxwell. The Maxwell House, or Maxwell Mansion, is the large two-building structure to the right of the Mill. What will become Lambert's Saloon is the second building to the right with the four windows in front. It is most probable that the saloon building was built by Lucien Maxwell also. Henry moves from Elizabethtown to Cimarron in late 1871 after Lucien Maxwell sold his land grant to the Maxwell Land Grant & Railway Company and moved to Fort Sumner, New Mexico.

As legend has it, Henry purchases the saloon in 1872. However, evidence has been found supporting his acquisition and operation of the saloon and inn in 1871. It is worth stating again, as mentioned in the 1907 book, *History of New Mexico-Anderson*, that Henry purchased a place from "the Grant" in the fall of 1871.

The Old Aztec Mill with the town of Cimarron in the distance circa 1866. What will become the Lambert Saloon is the small white building with the four windows in front. (Courtesy Audrey Alpers Collection)

This is expected to be the saloon, billiard parlor, and inn. Also, an original credit sheet showing expenses for the Maxwell Land Grant & Railway Company at Lambert's Saloon and Inn from 1871 has been discovered. This credit sheet clearly shows boarding for the MLG&RC men. Therefore, confirming that Henry was running a hotel or inn by December 1871.

Yet, there are still some curiosities with the property. After an exhaustive search in the Colfax Country records, two deeds/indentures were found in the county's deed books. Somewhere between 1872 and 1874, Joseph Holbrook (killer of David Crockett) enters into a lawsuit-judgment against the Maxwell Land Grand & Railway Company. This lawsuit goes to trial in early 1875 and is tried out of the District Court in and for the County of Santa Fe and Territory of New Mexico. The Court rules in favor of the plaintiff, Joseph Holbrook, and against the Maxwell Land Grant & Railway Company, defendant-debtor. The MLG&RC is forced to sell the Maxwell House along with the saloon and hotel properties to satisfy the debt, both of which Henry is occupying at that time. These properties were seized on April 10, 1875.

The question is, if Henry purchased the hotel in 1871 from the Grant, how can they sell it at auction in 1875? There are several possibilities. One being Henry enters into a personal note or a rent to own contract with the MLG&RC. This was very common in that era. Maxwell was said to have sold property to settlers on a handshake or an agreement written on the back of a napkin, only to be lost later. After searching the Colfax Country records, no evidence was found of any transaction between Henry and the MLG&RC on this property in 1871. This might indicate a personal note or agreement of some type was initiated.

The reason Henry would enter into a personal note with the MLG&RC may be surprisingly simple. Here is one theory. There was much turmoil with the MLG&RC and its legal boundaries after Maxwell sold the property in April of 1870. Soon afterward, the Maxwell Land Grant and Railway Company petitioned to get the grant approved by the U.S. government for roughly 2 million acres. However, the government approved the grant at only 97,000 acres. This was due to Mexican land grant law which stated a single land grant could be no more than 92,000 acres. This ruling and lack of income from the grant caused the MLG&RC to default on taxes. These legal proceedings would continue all the way to the U. S. Supreme Court where the court ruled a new survey be completed in 1876. The survey found the grant to contain 1,700,000 acres and the court issued a patent to the MLG&RC giving them full title to the land. All subsequent lawsuits finally ended in 1887 and the U.S. Supreme court ruled in favor of the grant.

When Joseph Holbrook entered into a lawsuit against the MLG&RC, the grant was short on cash and forced to call in all outstanding notes to satisfy the judgment. Henry, being the savvy businessman, realized he could buy the saloon and inn at auction cheaper than paying off the note, and this time with a legal deed. Of course, there could be other reasons, but this does show that Henry began operating and was occupying the saloon and hotel in 1871, not 1872.

On May 10, 1875, both of these properties were sold at public auction by Sheriff John C. Turner of Colfax County, Territory of New Mexico in front of the Cimarron Courthouse. The Maxwell House is sold in two parts, east and west, since there were two buildings on the property. The east side was the Maxwell family residence and the west side was used for entertaining, gambling, and servant's quarters. M.W. Mills was the highest bidder for the east side of the Maxwell House for Block A.W. Lots 6,7,8,9,10.

M.W. Mills' bid of $85.00 was over two-thirds of the appraised value of the property, as stated by the deed.

Also, on May 10, 1875, Henry is the highest bidder at $67.00 for Block A.W. Lots 2,3,4,5. This is the west side of the Maxwell House which Henry and his family are currently occupying as a dwelling house. Again, on May 10, 1875, Henry is the highest bidder at $102.00 for Block A.S.W. Lot 1. This is described in the deed papers, "in and to hold that certain lot or parcel of land lying and being situated in block A.S.W. Lot One (1) of the town plat of Cimarron together with all the buildings, improvements, and appurtenances thereto belonging and now being occupied by Henry Lambert as the St. James Hotel."

With this information, it is held that Henry purchased the saloon, billiard parlor, and inn from the MLG&RC in late 1871 and made improvements to the original saloon creating the St. James Hotel. Then, because of legal issues of the MLG&RC, Henry bought the property again in May 1875 at auction. The saloon, billiard parlor, and inn officially became the St. James Hotel somewhere in the late 1874 or early 1875 timeframe. From 1871 to 1874 it was known as Lambert's Saloon, Lambert's Place, or Lambert's Inn according to newspapers of the day. Henry and his family are living in the Maxwell House until late 1879 when the remodel is started on the St. James Hotel. More detail on this in Part 3 – The Addition.

One of the first cited accounts of the name "St. James Hotel" instead of Lambert's Saloon or Lambert's Inn was in the November 13, 1875, Las Vegas Gazette article on the Clay Allison shooting of Pancho Griego. It clearly states: "On Monday evening following the killing of Vega a difficulty occurred in the St. James Hotel between Griego and R. C. Allison in which Griego was shot and killed." This shows that the name "St. James Hotel" was formally in place prior to this event.

Lambert's Saloon

The original saloon which was called Lambert's Saloon, Lambert's Place, or Lambert's Inn as seen in the 1866 picture, was not a big structure. The building consisted of the main room (which is the present-day dining room and bar area). Inside the main room in the middle was a potbellied stove and a stone fireplace on the north wall by the bar. The original bar and back bar were in the northeast corner of the room against the east wall. The original bar was covered in sheet steel with a large mirror behind it. One story says Henry had a steel plate installed behind the front of the bar which served as protection for Henry when the shooting started. The back bar where liquor bottles were kept was below the bar height to keep bottles from getting shot during numerous gunfights. It was not the big beautiful wooden bar that comes after the addition in 1880.

The entrance to the saloon and billiard parlor (the main room) was on the west side of the building on Collinson Avenue (named for John Collinson, the principal stockholder in the Maxwell Land Grant and Railway Company), which also doubled as part of the Santa Fe Trail. The entry consisted of two full-size double doors. There were no swinging batwing doors. In the main room were also a roulette table, monte table, and a poker table. These were in the northwest corner of the main room. On the south side of the main room was a large billiard table. The cue rack and tally board for pen pool were mounted on the south wall. Pen pool was a popular game played on the billiard table in these days. This billiard table would have numerous bodies laid upon it after the many shootings that took place in the St. James.

Beyond the main room on the south side were two private gambling rooms. Each private gambling room had its own door. One door close to the east wall and one door close to the west wall. These were locked during the poker games. The rooms were not bothered unless a gambler came to the door asking for drinks, normally after a poker round was finished. There was a slot in the middle of each poker table in these private gambling rooms where a blue chip would be dropped to keep track of the rounds of drinks. To rent these rooms it was $25.00 a night and $1.00 per round of drinks. The winner of the night would pick up the tab.

On the north side beyond the main room was the dining room where Henry served his famous dishes such as pork sherry tenderloin, pureed carrots, and roasted potatoes. It is said Henry only cooked with fine wines and he used no water when he cooked his well-known dishes. To the east side of the dining room was a small washroom, between it and the saloon was a narrow hall that led to the kitchen. The kitchen was on the east side beyond the main saloon room.

During the reopening of the St. James Hotel in the mid-1980s by then owner Ed Sitzberger, the original stove foundation for Henry's kitchen was found. Back in the 1800s stoves were made of cast iron or steel, therefore weighed hundreds of pounds and tended not to hold up well on wooden floors. Stoves were placed on stone or similar foundations so they could be stabilized and not be at risk of going through the floor because of the weight. Also, stoves in this era burned on wood or coal and embers would fall out onto the floor occasionally. This way the embers would fall onto the stone foundation and not a wood floor, possibly causing a fire.

The stove foundation was found in what is today's café, just to the southeast of the host station. This is where Henry's original kitchen was. Also, in the same time period, a second stove foundation was found behind the current day wooden bar. This is where the kitchen had been moved when Ed reopened the St. James in 1985. When the kitchen was moved is unknown.

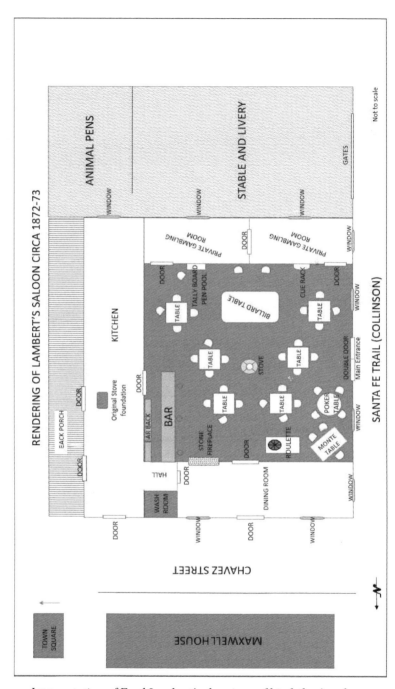

Interpretation of Fred Lambert's drawings of his father's saloon.

In the saloon, there was a large print of a maiden, a sea monster, and a hero that hung on the wall. This print was an advertisement for J. Hostetter's Stomach Bitters. After ingesting some "fire water" or "Taos lightning," the cowboys would shoot at the sea monster in the print trying to help the young hero. Eventually, the print became so shot up it was beyond repair. Fred Lambert made a detailed sketch which included the bullet holes and wrote a poem about the picture. These are now on display in the Old Aztec Mill Museum.

In 1901, Henry Lambert's sons, Fred and Gene, repaired the ceiling in the original saloon. They found over 400 bullets above the bar. The reason no one was killed in the rooms above the saloon is that there was a double layer of thick wood that stopped the bullets. Today, in the dining room ceiling (the old saloon) there are still 22 bullet holes in the pressed tin ceiling. It is highly likely that there are hundreds of bullets still embedded in the walls.

The Picture

by Fred Lambert

I wish to tell you a story

  When the west was wild and young,

About in the old ad and picture

  That in Lambert's bar room hung.

The picture was in gay colors

  But now all faded and bullet riddled it be,

In tinseled letters there was a verse

  That ALL COMERS could read and see:

"THE GREAT HOME CELEBRATED HOSTETTER'S BITTERS,

  NOW, LISTEN TO WHAT I HAVE TO SAY

GUARANTEED NINTY-SIX PERCENT ALCOHOL

  AND WILL DRIVE ALL DULL CARES AWAY."

The picture was of a rocky bluff

  On a seashore with waves running high,

A beautiful maiden chained to the rocks

  A sea serpent with red and blazing eyes.

From the rocky bluff far above her

Her lover leaps with a shining spear,

To kill the deadly sea serpent

And save his sweetheart filled with fear.

Often some old lanky cow puncher

In town on a spree and tare

Would glance up at that picture

Then loudly commence to rant and swear

Quickly pull his six gun from the holster

Take a cool and deliberate aim,

Pumping lead into the deadly sea serpent

Then turning to the bartender would exclaim:

Guess as how that feller needed help

Before that animule reached the gal,

"Bartender...Why'd they have her chained there

Couldn't they keep her in the Home Corral?"

Picture of Fred Lambert's drawing of the advertisement for J. Hostetter's Stomach Bitters which hung in the St. James Saloon. He even copied the bullet holes in the picture. (Courtesy Old Aztec Mill Museum)

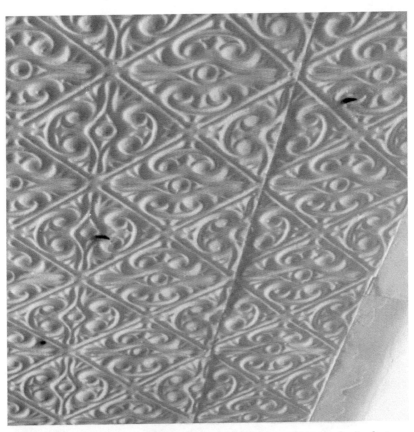

Bullet holes in the pressed tin ceiling inside the saloon, today's dining and bar area. (Author's collection)

The Wild West Years and the Killings

--- "It appears Lambert had himself another man for breakfast"

This was a popular saying in Cimarron following a killing at Lambert's Saloon the night before. It is said 26 people were killed or died in the St. James Hotel and Saloon. Each of them a violent death. Though only 17 (not counting family members) can be documented, it is very likely that more died or were killed in the St. James. Their stories were not noted and therefore lost with time.

Lambert had a sign posted over the back of his bar that stated:

> *"Gents Will Please Leave Their Six-Gun Behind the Bar While in Town. This Will Lessen the Customary Collection for Burials."*

List of those killed or died in Lambert's Saloon and St. James Hotel, Cimarron, Territory of New Mexico from 1872 to 1884.

These incidents, names, and dates were taken from articles in the Santa Fe, Las Vegas, Springer, Elizabethtown, and Cimarron newspapers along with Henry Lambert's eyewitness accounts of these killings passed down to his son Fred Lambert and additional sources.

3 – Buffalo Soldiers Killed by David "Davy" Crockett and Gus Heffron – March 24, 1876

1 – Monte Dealer Juan Borrego Killed by David "Davy" Crockett – Prior to September 1876

1 – Ranchero Francisco "Pancho" Griego Killed by Clay Allison – November 1, 1875

1 – John Black Killed by Clay Allison – May 21, 1872

1 – Marshal John Wilson Killed by Clay Allison – Unable to verify the date

1 – Gambler Pomeroy Laughlin Killed by Wall Henderson - May 11, 1872

1 – Juan Benito Archuleta Killed by Henry Lambert – September 6, 1879

2 – Cattle Rustlers Killed by Sheriff Rinehart – Unable to verify the date (Rinehart's term as Sheriff was between 1876-77)

1 – Bill Curren Killed by Bob Ford, Dick Liddil, Chas Walker or Wall Henderson – about 1884

1 – Charles Morris Killed by Chunk Colbert – July 23, 1872

1 – Feliciano Butarus Killed by Sam Tipton – Unable to verify the date

1- Soldier Killed and 2 Wounded – Soldiers from Fort Union 6th Cav., Co. G. Private Shian (shot and killed), Private Carroll (shot, wounded), Private Gately (stabbed in the back, wounded) by Francisco "Pancho" Griego – May 31, 1875

Other deaths in the St. James Hotel

1 – Prairie Dog Payne shot a Mr. Shook three times in the chest in E. Charette's saloon across the street. Shook made it to the St. James Hotel and died the following morning in room 6.

1 – Charles Love, a C. S. Ranch cowboy, riding with a posse that fought against the Black Jack Ketchum Gang in Turkey Canyon. Love is shot through the rear hip, but he had a pocketknife in his rear pocket which he had used in sticking black leg cattle. Blood poisoning sets in and he dies in the St. James room 2.

Family members that died in the St. James Hotel:

- Anna Elizabeth (Mollie/Mary) Stepp Lambert in 1881

- Johnny Lambert (son of Henry & Mary Elizabeth Lambert) in 1892

- Henry Lambert in 1913

Narratives of Gunfights and Killings

Buffalo Soldiers Killed by David "Davy" Crockett and Gus Heffron – March 24, 1876

David John "Davy" Crockett was born in Tennessee in 1853 and is said to be related to "Davy Crockett of the Alamo." He was a southerner and loyal to the Confederacy. He did not like Yankee soldiers and especially not Buffalo Yankee soldiers. The story told in the Las Vegas Gazette on April 1, 1876, has three soldiers coming to Henry's saloon and getting into a disagreement with two cowboys, David Crockett and Gus Heffron. The soldiers left the saloon for their camp outside of Cimarron. After lights out, they returned to the saloon. Upon entering, the hostilities were resumed. Some twenty shots were fired. All of the Buffalo soldiers were killed. One soldier died falling into a corner by the gaming tables in a sitting posture clutching his revolver. A total of nine shots were found lodged in the three soldiers. Their remains were brought back to Fort Union.

In a report to the Assistant Adjunct General, Department of Missouri, requests to deal with civil disturbances were made because of the presence of a large lawless element in Cimarron. With the inability of local authorities to keep the peace, the Attorney General of New Mexico Territory, under the direction of Governor Marsh Giddings, requested troops from Fort Union to help Sheriff Isaiah Rinehart restore order in Cimarron. After the three soldiers were killed at Cimarron, more troops were sent from Fort Union.

Company L, Ninth Cavalry, were sent to Cimarron on March 26, 1876. Crockett and Heffron avoided capture until the summer when the two men were arrested and charged with the murder of the three soldiers. Crockett and Heffron stood trial but were released due to a lack of evidence. A Las Vegas Gazette article stated, "they were discharged of the murder of the three negro soldiers, by a weak Justice of the Peace."

The same article from the Gazette said Crockett and Heffron were, "becoming emboldened and determined to become notorious." In September of the same year, cornered by Colfax County Sheriff Isaiah "Ike" Rinehart and Deputy Joe Holbrook on a citizen's complaint, Crockett and Heffron were both shot. Crockett was shot by Deputy Holbrook and died from his wounds at a house nearby soon afterward. Heffron, though wounded, got away. He was later captured. As the story goes, Crockett, while sitting on his horse, dared Deputy Holbrook to shoot him. Holbrook, in turn, emptied both barrels into Crockett. The papers said Crockett was an individual of "no particular calling, save outlaw."

The next afternoon, October 1, 1876, Crockett was "very respectfully" buried somewhere in the Cimarron Cemetery. A hand-drawn map of the Cimarron Cemetery, later named Mountain View Cemetery, was found dating back to the early 1970s created by a local historian Frank Alpers. Mr. Alpers meticulously drew a scaled map of the cemetery noting all markers and listing the names on headstones and wooden markers that were still legible. Crockett's wooden headboard was not on the map. From the map, we can get a sense of the general area where he was buried because of other markers of the same era. The only hint we have is from New Mexico historian F. Stanley's book *One Half Mile from Heaven...The Cimarron Story-1949* and his book *Desperados of New Mexico-1953* including a picture of the possible gravesite. It is suggested that Crockett is buried somewhere near Reverend Tolby's grave. This would be feasible as it was rumored that Crockett was part of the lynch mob that hung Reverend Tolby's killer. It may have been considered a place of honor being buried close to Reverend Tolby. Crockett's friend Clay Allison most likely chose where Crockett was buried.

Allison had a grave marker made at the A. H. Carey hardware store, but a person claiming to be a relative of Crockett took the marker many years ago stating the wooden headboard was unsuitable and would replace it with a marble headstone. The town council allowed the marker to be taken. Neither the marker nor the person who took it have been seen since. Nothing marks the grave now but weeds.

Note: There is an additional story of five Buffalo Soldiers being shot and killed by Clay Allison and David Crockett in the St. James Hotel at an unknown date. Yet another story of Crockett killing five soldiers by himself. Although it is mentioned in Fred Lambert's notes and a newspaper article from the 1950s or 1960s in Fred's possession, after a detailed search among military and communication records from Fort Union and other sources, there is no mention of the five soldiers being killed. These records do have both incidents of soldiers being killed by David Crockett and Gus Heffron, along with Francisco "Pancho" Griego and are mentioned in detailed reports to commanding officers. Also, research was done on Clay Allison's life to find this story with negative results. Because of this, it is suspected the story of the five soldiers being killed by Crockett and Allison or Crockett alone are variations of the story above of Crockett and Heffron.

Monte Dealer Juan Borrego Killed by David "Davy" Crockett

This account was passed down from father to son. The story was hand drawn on a piece of paper by Fred Lambert and witnessed by his father, Henry. Apparently, Borrego was dealing a game of "find the lady" or "three-card Monte" at the St. James. Monte is a card version of the old "shell game" and the "mark" or "victim" against a seasoned con artist has almost no chance of winning. Crockett, who got very mean when drunk, protested to losing the trick. After an argument, both men went for their guns and Crockett shot first. Borrego lie dead on the floor.

Ranchero Francisco "Pancho" Griego Killed by Clay Allison – November 1, 1875

R.C. "Clay" Allison was a man with a big smile and was often quick to buy drinks at the bar. He owned a ranch not far from Cimarron, where he would come to town often with his cowboys. Allison was involved in the Colfax County War where the new owners of the Maxwell Land Grant, the Maxwell Land Grant and Railway Company, a Dutch/English Investment firm were bullying homesteaders on the grant. The Company was allied with Governor Axtell and the Santa Fe Ring. The Santa Fe Ring was also involved in the Lincoln County War. The main defender of the homesteaders was Reverend F.J. Tolby. Reverend Tolby was assassinated on September 14, 1875. The 33-year-old minister was found shot in the back in Cimarron Canyon for his outspokenness against the grant owners and politicians. Rumor had it that Cruz Vega was involved in the murder. On Sunday evening October 30, 1875, a masked mob that was believed to be led by Clay Allison hung Vega on a telegraph pole.

Francisco "Pancho" Griego, who was alleged to be Vega's uncle, claimed the body and vowed vengeance. To make matters worse, two days later, on November 1, 1875, Allison interrupted the burial of Vega telling Griego he would not allow his nephew to be buried in the same cemetery as the man he had killed, Reverend Tolby. This forced Griego to bury Vega outside the city limits in the potter's field. Later that evening after the burial, Pancho Griego who had been making threats against Allison all day found Clay in the saloon of the St. James Hotel. What happened next is best described by the editor of the Santa Fe New Mexican newspaper:

"On the night of November 1st, Francisco Griego was shot and killed by Clay Allison. Both parties met at the door of the St. James Hotel (Lambert's), entered, and with some friends took a drink when the two walked into the corner of the room and had some conversation. There Allison drew his revolver and shot three times. The lights were extinguished and Griego was not found until the next morning. Francisco Griego was well known in Santa Fe, where his mother lives. He has killed a great many men and was considered a dangerous man; few regret his loss."

Francisco "Pancho" Griego was buried in Cimarron, but in 1877 his remains were reinterred to Santa Fe where his mother and family lived (The Weekly New Mexican, November 16, 1877). He is buried in Rosario Cemetery, Santa Fe, New Mexico.

Note: Reverend Tolby's original headstone was found as a stepping stone in the back of the St. James Hotel in the 1990s by then owner Ed Sitzberger. It is unknown exactly when it was placed there, but it would have been after the larger and more ornate monument was erected. This headstone is now on display in the St. James Hotel.

Headstone of Francisco "Pancho" Griego – Rosario Cemetery, Santa Fe, New Mexico. The headstone reads: IN MEMORY OF FRANSISCO GRIEGO KILLED THE 1ST DAY OF NOVEMBER 1875 AT THE AGE OF 38 YEARS, PRAY FOR __. The phrase is assumed to be "Pray for him." This phrase is possible scripture. The "HIM" has been stricken from the headstone for some reason. (Author's Collection).

John Black Killed by Clay Allison – May 21, 1872

John Black, who was only 18 years of age, came to Cimarron claiming he had killed 14 men. Clay Allison heard his bragging and sat down with him inside Henry's saloon. Allison ordered two coffees and two six shooters. The young fellow went for his gun first, but Clay beat him to the draw. Later the jury exonerated him from all charges. John Black is buried in the Cimarron Cemetery. His is one of the first graves on the left (east of the road) as you drive into the cemetery and has a large rounded, very weathered headboard. The headboard, almost one hundred and fifty years old now, is barely legible and very fragile. The following picture was taken in 1990 by the author. It reads: *IN MEMORY OF JOHN BLACK, DIED MAY 21, 1872, AGED 18 YEARS, MAY HIS SOUL REST IN PEACE.* Today, unfortunately, is it so weathered it is almost unreadable.

Marshal John Wilson Killed by Clay Allison

This shooting was also mentioned in Fred Lambert's notes. There is confusion here as Cimarron did not introduce a Town Marshal until the 1900s and Clay Allison left Cimarron in 1877. The first Cimarron Town Marshal was Fred Lambert, Henry's son, who was elected and won by one vote in 1911. From 1872 to 1882 Cimarron was the county seat and that is where the Sheriff's office was located. The men that held the Sheriff position between 1870 to 1881 were: Andrew J. Calhoun (1869-71); Orson K. Chittenden (1871-73); John C. Turner (1873-75); Orson K. Chittenden (1875-76, Governor Axtell removed Chittenden from office and appointed Rinehart); Isaiah "Ike" Rinehart (1876-77); Peter Burleson (1877-80), and Allen C. Wallace (1881-83, he was the last Sheriff of Colfax County seat in Cimarron). Mason "Mace" Bowman, feared for his fast draw even by Clay Allison, was a Deputy Sheriff under Wallace when the county seat moved to

Weathered headboard of John Black – Cimarron Cemetery, Cimarron, New Mexico. Picture was taken in 1990. (Author's Collection)

Springer, New Mexico in 1881 and became Sheriff afterward. Mace died of natural causes after less than a year in office. John Wilson was not mentioned as a Sheriff in this timeframe. He could have possibly been a Deputy Sheriff, Constable, or in another law enforcement position.

A similar mention of this event was in a small booklet about Cimarron, New Mexico published in the 1940s found in the Raton Library. This booklet states: "The Marshal and Henry Lambert were talking in Lambert's saloon when Clay Allison came in. The Marshal, understanding how raucous Clay got when he had a few drinks, tried to talk him out of the bottle. During the conversation, the Marshal took off his hat and held it in front of him at waist level. Within the blink of an eye, Clay Allison reached for his Colt and shot the Marshal, killing him. Allison claimed the Marshal was reaching for his gun behind his hat and he had shot him in self-defense. Clay was acquitted." This story did not mention the Marshal by name.

Another version of this story is in the 1931 Stuart Lake, Wyatt Earp biography, *Wyatt Earp Frontier Marshal*. There the story is almost identical, but names the Marshal as "Marshal Pancho, a well-known frontier peace officer."

Note: These stories could also be confused with the Pancho Griego shooting or the killing of Bent County Deputy Sheriff and Constable Charles Faber in Las Animas, Colorado. Allison shot and killed Faber after he and his Deputies tried to arrest Allison and his brother John, for not checking their guns while in town. Again, Clay was acquitted.

Gambler Pomeroy Laughlin Killed by Wall Henderson - May 11, 1872

This was documented by Fred Lambert through his father Henry, as he was a witness to this killing. There are little details of the shooting, but Fred left a hand-drawn sketch of this event. Most likely what happened here, as in typical gambling related fights, one accused the other of cheating. In this case, Pomeroy Laughlin lost.

Wall Henderson was a miner from Elizabethtown and ended up killing some men who tried to jump his claim. After this trouble, Henderson gave up his claim and began to drink heavily. He then became associated with unsavory characters within the region. Henderson said he had eight notches on one side of his gun for the men he had wounded and seven notches on the other side for the men he had killed. He was always looking for a fight saying he wanted to "even up" both sides of his gun. He became a hated braggart in Colfax County. Looking for trouble eventually caught up with him and he was shot and killed. Wall Henderson is buried in the Elizabethtown, New Mexico Cemetery.

Laughlin is buried in Cimarron Cemetery and is one of the first graves on the left as you drive into the cemetery. It is the first one past the rounded headboard of John Black. The marker read: *In Memory of Pomeroy Laughlin, Native of Ohio, Died in Cimarron May 11, 1872, Age 32 years.* The wooden marker, now being almost a hundred and fifty years old, is broken and lying on the ground. It is worn and illegible. A small metal cross also marks the grave.

Juan Benito Archuleta Killed by Henry Lambert – September 6, 1879

The Cimarron News & Press and the Las Vegas Daily Gazette reported that Juan Benito Archuleta, being under the influence of liquor, was abusing Henry Lambert in his hotel. Henry knocked Archuleta down and he struck his head on the stone fireplace by the bar rupturing an artery. He died a few hours later.

Cattle Rustlers Killed by Sheriff Rinehart

This shooting was also mentioned in Fred Lambert's notes. Sheriff Isaiah "Ike" Rinehart was sheriff of Colfax County in the 1876-77 timeframe. Little details of this event are known.

Bill Curren Killed by Bob Ford, Dick Liddil, Chas Walker or Wall Henderson

Sometime in 1884, Bob Ford and Dick Liddil arrived in Cimarron. This is the same Bob Ford that killed Jesse James and Dick Liddil was a former member of the James Gang. They stayed at the St. James for several days. During this time, they engaged in poker games into the early hours of the morning. One particular night Ford and Liddil were playing poker with Chas Walker, Bill Curren, and Wall Henderson. As the sun started to come up the players were tired and cranky after a long night of poker. A quarrel broke out over who should pay for the night's entertainment. Guns were quickly drawn, and shots fired…smoke filled the room. Everyone walked out the door except Bill Curren, who lie dead on the floor. The four men never told which of them killed Curren and they all took that secret to their graves.

Charles Morris Killed by Chunk Colbert – July 23, 1872

This is another incident told to Fred by his father, Henry, who witnessed the killing. This account is told in Fred Lambert's own words from his notes:

"Morris was from Colorado. Had come to Cimarron with Chunk Colbert's wife. One day, Chunk Colbert showed up at Lambert's saloon looking for Charles Morris. Morris was drinking at the bar when Colbert stepped up and said; 'I understand that you have something that used to belong to me, naturally you need killing for enticing my wife away.' Morris tried to make a quick draw, but Colbert shot first and Morris dropped to the floor with 'lead poisoning.'"

Morris is buried in Cimarron Cemetery and is one of the first graves on the left as you drive into the cemetery. It is the second one past the rounded headboard of John Black. The marker read: *Charles Morris, Native of Tennessee, Died in Cimarron July 23, 1872, Age 32 Years.* The wooden marker has decayed, and the grave is unmarked.

Colbert held a record of having killed seven men and was considered a tough hombre up around Trinidad, Colorado. Later, Clay Allison killed him at the Clifton House over a horse race. Of course, Clay was exonerated.

Feliciano Butarus Killed by Sam Tipton

This is another incident told to Fred by his father, Henry, who witnessed the killing. Fred mentions that this story is in a "Maxwell Manuscript." This account is told in Fred Lambert's own words from his notes:

"Feliciano Butarus, who, when a boy, had been captured by the Comanche Indians in old Mexico near Chihuahua. He was captured when he was about seven years old and lived with the Comanche for 20 years when he took the notion to return to the Mexicans. Feliciano, though a Mexican by birth, was a real Comanche in actions. His 20 years of training made him an equal, if not superior to the Comanche Indians as a horseman. He had picked up a little English, could speak Spanish, and understood several Indian dialects.

One day Feliciano Butarus rode up to the St. James Corral, he had three fine horses that he had stolen from Sam Tipton down at Watrous. He had made the sale of two horses to Lucien Maxwell and was dealing with Henry Lambert for the third when Tipton and another cowman named McAllister rode up to the corral, tied their horses and came on into the saloon. Butarus recognized Tipton as the owner of the horses and made a quick dash toward the dining room. Tipton missed his first shot but took another at Butarus as he was crossing the street, felling him near the entrance to the Maxwell House. They carried him back to the St. James bar and laid him out on the billiard table where he died.

They hired two Mexicans to bury him. They had a little spring wagon and after a few rounds of drinks started for the cemetery. They had just crossed the arroyo and started up the hill when one of the tires came off the wheel and spokes flew in all directions. So, they decided to bury him right there on the hillside."

Soldier from Fort Union 6th Cav., Killed by Francisco "Pancho" Griego. Two Others Wounded – June 6, 1875

This is another incident told to Fred by his father, Henry, who witnessed the killing. This account is told in Fred Lambert's own words from his notes:

"Pancho Griego was dealing Monte in Lambert's saloon. A number of soldiers from Fort Union were bucking-the-game. The dispute arose over one of the heavy bets. The Monte Table was tipped over and Griego drew his pistol and Bowie knife and commenced firing at the soldiers...then ran toward the front door. Private Shian dropped at the first shot, Private Gately was stabbed in the back and dropped dead. Private Carrol was shot to death as he ran through the door toward their horses which were tied at the hitch rack in front of the saloon."

After further research, this story is not accurate. According to the Las Vegas Gazette of June 5, 1875, and The Weekly New Mexican June 8, 1875, a dispute occurred during a monte game, where several soldiers of the Sixth Cavalry were being dealt by Griego. An argument ensued over a lost bet and a soldier grabbed for the money. Griego collected the rest of the money and a soldier tried to take it from him. Griego pulled his six-shooter and knife and the soldiers ran for the door. Shots were fired by Griego hitting Private Shian killing him. Private Gately was shot in the hip and Private Carroll was cut in the back. All of this occurred by the front door of the St. James. Francisco "Pancho" Griego escaped but would be killed later that year by Clay Allison. This event was also mentioned in military communications reports from Fort Union (Fort Union Historic Resources Study).

Mountain View Cemetery Cimarron, N.M., old section marked with grave sites of prominent deaths (Google Maps).

The West Was Really Wild

The law of the gun was real as told in these stories. Some men were lawless and had little regard for human life. The scales of justice did not always balance in the west, as it was hard to stand up for what was right when looking down the barrel of a gun. Western law was also served at the end of a rope with just a hint or rumor of the victim's guilt by unruly drunken mobs led by men who danced on the head of the pin between justice and injustice.

The west was really wild. It was a ruthless teacher and could sense the weak. The west respected those who were strong and steadfast but pushed character to the limit. For those who were not...the west was a cruel disciplinarian. The Spanish word Cimarron means wild, untamed, unbroken, an accurate description of the early days of Cimarron, New Mexico.

Las Vegas (New Mexico) Gazette, November 18, 1875:

"-Cimarron is becoming a decidedly interesting neighborhood and Life Insurance Companies are instructing agents not to take any more risks in that section."

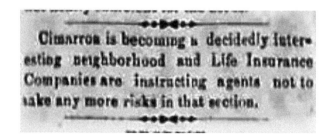

Part 3: The Addition

Henry's Grand Hotel

Important note: *Much of this part has direct statements from legal documents such as deeds, indentures, and letters of agreement. All of these documents are in 1880s legalese and can be a challenge to read. These were put into the book to give a feel for the era and for the pertinent information they contain. These sections will be contained within "quotation" marks. A loose summary is added before or after these statements.*

On November 17, 1879, Henry enters into an "Articles of Agreement" with Frank R. Sherwin to arrange the purchase of the remainder of the block and lots around the St. James Hotel currently owned by the Maxwell Land Grant and Railway Company. Frank R. Sherwin is the Manager of the Maxwell Land Grant and Railway Company. He too enters into this agreement and would be party to the first part, for himself and on behalf of bondholders represented by him. Henry Lambert is the party of the second part, and for the sum of $1.00 in hand enters into the "Articles of Agreement" with the MLG&RC.

Colfax County records Mortgage Book 'A': "Witnesseth, that the said party of the first part for and in consideration of the sum of $1.00 to him in hand paid the receipt whereof is hereby acknowledged, and in further consideration of the payments and covenants to be paid and performed as is here after mentioned has contracted and agreed to sell and convey unto the party of the second part his heirs and assigns all of that certain four lots or parcels of land lying and being in the town of Cimarron, County and Territory aforesaid, known and distinguished by and from the map and [1]plat of said as made and platted by the Maxwell Land Grant and Railway Company designated thereon as lots one, two, three, and four in Block A.S.W. The same fronting on the Street known as [2]Barlow Avenue and the corner lot number one bordering on the street known as Chavez Street together with all buildings thereon the same being occupied by the second party (Henry) and all appurtenances thereto anywise belonging."

[1]The town of Cimarron was platted by the MLG&RC between 1875 and 1879.

[2]This is a mistake as the property did not front Barlow, but Collinson Avenue (today called Collison Avenue).

The articles of agreement go on to say that the Maxwell Land Grant and Railway Company will deliver a good and sufficient deed for the said four lots and parcels of land described above for the sum of $2,250.00. And that Henry agrees to pay the mortgage to the MLG&RC of $2,250.00 on or before the expiration of 10 years from the date of the said deed bearing interest of seven percent annually. It also agrees that Henry shall build a new commodious (large & spacious) hotel as it is to be hereinafter provided upon said lots. It also states that should the first party (MLG&RC) fail, neglect or refuse to comply with the covenants in agreements herein contracted will provide the title to said lots or parcels of land and will pay a penalty sum of $5,000.00 or the actual damages sustained by the party of the second part (Henry).

"It is also agreed and understood that the said second party (Henry) agrees to surrender and deliver possession of the portion of the Maxwell House as occupied by him for hotel purposes on the north side of the street from where the above described lots or parcels of land are situated upon the opposite of the same street together with all appurtenances thereunto belonging and that all right or title of said second party thereto is hereby sold and conveyed to said first party forever it being understood and agreed that the said second party will occupy the premises hereby contracted to be sold henceforth under these articles as of his own property free from any charges or veil, and it being further understood that said second party will secure and free of charges or veil the large stone building opposite on the other side of the street from the premises hereby contracted to be sold for said the second party to be by him used in connection with hotel for sleeping rooms to the same as the above portion of the Maxwell House so to be vacated by said second party has heretofore last used."

"The said second party also promises and agrees to and with the said first party that he will build or cause to be built a large and commodious hotel upon the said above premises contracted to be sold and that the cost of the same shall not be less than $4000 in the construction thereof it being understood that the construction thereof will be made complete as near as may be within one year from the making and executing of said deed and that possession of the said stone building shall continue until July 1st next following a date of these articles and when it is expected the said hotel building so to be constructed will be sufficiently completed that the said second party may occupy the same for sleeping rooms etc., and it will be prepared and ready to vacate in surrender possession of said stone building."

These document sections are very interesting as they state Henry would deliver possession of the west portion of the Maxwell House which he purchased in 1875 to the MLG&RC. In exchange, they will allow him to occupy the large stone building, which is believed to be the Aztec Mill, until the addition to the St. James Hotel is ready to occupy. Henry and family are occupying the west section of the Maxwell House which includes a row of the rooms that were used as servant's quarters by Maxwell. It is possible these rooms were used as overflow from the actual St. James Hotel or as more permanent rental housing for locals.

Originally, the east section of the Maxwell House was used as family quarters for the Maxwells. This section burned down in 1888. The west section was the guest quarters, gambling room, and servant's sleeping rooms which burned in 1924. There is a wonderful model of the Maxwell House in the Old Aztec Mill Museum which gives a great visual.

These sections of the "articles" also show that the Maxwell Land Grant and Railway Company had a vested interest and is believed to be in a partnership with Henry to build this new and larger St. James Hotel in Cimarron. This is most likely due to the MLG&RC speculating that the railroad will reach Cimarron soon and the town will be in need of a luxurious hotel. The actual property sale agreed to in the "Articles of Agreement" is not formalized by deed until September 10, 1880, and also states that Henry at that time paid off the promissory note: "the indenture between the Maxwell Land Grant and Railway Company a corporation duly organized, constituted, and existing under and by virtue of the laws and the kingdom of the Netherlands and doing business with the territory of New Mexico - receipt of payment of sum ($2,250.00) in hand is acknowledged and has granted release of land, lots, parcels and tracts, - Block A.S.W. Lots 1,2,3,4."

The deed is in both Henry Lambert's and Mollie (Mary Stepp) Lambert's name. This is one month before her death.

Note: It is again worth mentioning that Henry's first wife Anna Elizabeth Stepp liked to use the nicknames Mollie and Mary, although in all legal documentation she only used the name "Mollie." The only places the name "Mary" can be found are in the 1880 census and her headstone.

The west section of the Maxwell Mansion. Henry and Mary (Stepp) lived in this as a residence for several years until the addition to the hotel was started in 1880. Notice the plaster has a faux stone block look. Circa 1924 post-fire. (Courtesy Audrey Alpers Collection)

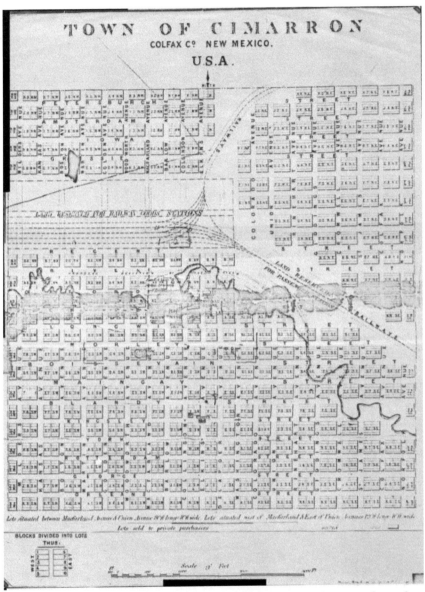

A copy of weathered circa 1875 Town of Cimarron plot map from the Maxwell Land Grant & Railway Company. You will notice the land designated for the railroad in the middle of town. The railroad did not get to Cimarron until the early 1900's. (Author's collection)

Newspaper Accounts of Construction

Construction of the addition to the original saloon and hotel started in January 1880. Henry's dream was to build a grand hotel rivaling the hotels in the east. Everyone was excited about this new hotel. Even local and area newspapers kept track of the construction progress. The Cimarron News and Press reported on the building of the hotel for almost two years.

Cimarron News and Press, November 20, 1879

"Henry Lambert made a satisfactory arrangement for the purchase of the building he is now occupying, and the four lots adjoining each other on that block. Mr. Henry Lambert will proceed to erect a handsome building for a hotel. He informs us that as soon as spring opened, he would raise the present building one story higher. It will have a north front 90 feet long, extending to the alley. His present stables will be torn down at once and an icehouse, granary, storeroom, and stables will be commenced forthwith. He will probably spend six or seven thousand dollars in improving his present property, which will then make a very handsome appearance."

Cimarron News and Press, January 22, 1880

"Henry Lambert has 50 or 60 loads of excellent buildings stone deliver preparatory to laying a foundation for his new hotel."

Cimarron News and Press, March 18, 1880

"Progress on the Lambert hotel is being a little delayed awaiting the arrival of some $2000 worth of material from Chicago."

Las Vegas Daily Gazette August 4, 1880

"Col. Lockhart is shipping lumber by the car load from his lumber yard in New Town. Yesterday he was engaged in filling five cars with flooring and other kinds of dressed lumber. Four of these cars are destined for Bernalillo, Albuquerque and Las Lunas, while the fifth is to be sent to Henry Lambert, at Springer."

Las Vegas Daily Gazette, December 9, 1880

"Cimarron News and Press: Work on the St James hotel is being pushed forward as rapidly as the cold weather will permit, and in a short time Cimarron can boast of as fine a hotel, if not the finest, of any place in New Mexico. The building, a two story one, is in the form of an "L". The downstairs is occupied by the kitchen, dining room, billiard room, two club rooms and the washrooms, all in the south wing, while in the east wing are the offices, one suite, and five single sleeping rooms. Upstairs are the parlors, four suites, and eleven sleeping rooms, together with four bathrooms. In the rooms throughout are all hard finished and are furnished with gas pipes so that at any time all that will have to be done will be connect the building to the mains. The suites, connected by sliding doors, are fitted with stationary washstands that supply hot and cold water. When complete an iron balcony will extend along the sides of the building facing the streets. Some few of the rooms are already furnished and occupied and it will not be long before all will be ready for the reception of guests."

Note from the author: After numerous walk-throughs and examinations of the hotel with former owner, Ed Sitzberger, it is believed the above article is not completely accurate. For instance, even though the hotel has been updated over the years there are no traces of any sliding doors between suites. Also, an iron balcony was never built. However, a wooden balcony was built sometime after the turn of the century, some 20 years later. It is possible that the original design may have changed for numerous reasons.

Las Vegas Daily Gazette May 4, 1881

"Henry Lambert is doing the most for the town at present. He has erected a large two-story adobe hotel containing 28 rooms and is now engaged in finishing and plastering inside and out. The hotel is furnished with hot and cold baths, upstairs and down. It is to be lighted with gas or gasoline as circumstances will permit. Ed McCaffrey is doing the plastering. The hothouse has been arranged and some beautiful plants were now growing. When finished this will be one of the best hotels in the territory."

Note: The hothouse is a greenhouse and was located at the end of the south wing (a one-story addition).

Cimarron News and Press, August 16, 1881

"Mr. Henry Lambert has engaged in painter "A. Desmonts" who is doing some fine ornamental painting on the inside wood work of the St. James."

Inside the St. James

The foundation for the hotel was made of large stones and its walls were made of adobe bricks two feet thick. Stucco and plaster were applied to the exterior and interior to seal the adobe. Large windows were in every room to give plenty of light and the outside of the windows was wrapped in hand-carved wood molding. The roof of the hotel was trimmed in ornate metal cornice. Many of these elements are still visible today.

A large portion of the material for the hotel and its interior was transported by railroad, then wagon from back east. There was a coal fireplace or stove in every room along with a large poster bed, a marble-topped dresser, and tables. All the fireplaces were hand built with custom mantels. The fireplaces had small burning areas which would point toward the use of coal, plus there was coal in the Dawson area some miles to the north for easy supply. Decorative mirrors hung above the fireplaces. Many rooms and suites had marble sinks which can still be seen in some rooms. There were at least two copper bathtubs in the washrooms. The copper tubs have long since vanished.

The hotel had the finest of everything including dinnerware, silverware, drapes, tablecloths, furniture, and other embellishments. In the parlor, there was a love seat, dark red plush drapes, and a grand piano. The walls were decorated with fine paintings and etchings. The floors were all hardwood and the trim hand carved. Ornate rugs covered the floors. Marble busts even adorned some rooms and lavish wallpaper covered the walls. Several etchings and two original dinner bells are on display at the Old Aztec Mill Museum.

As mentioned before, Henry hired painter A. Desmonts to hand paint the wood interior of the hotel. He painted greenery above the doors and murals on the walls of mountain scenes and trees. He even painted blank wooden doors and the doorways to look like beautifully grained wood. Most of these painted doors and doorways are still on the upper floor. The painting of these doors is noticeable if you look closely.

Even the bar area was given a makeover in efforts to ignore its violent past and promote the new elegant atmosphere of the hotel. A new bar and back bar were brought in. The new bar was an opulent hand-carved wooden piece. A far cry from the sheet-steel original and added much class to the room. According to a picture from the Lambert family that was passed down from Mary Elizabeth, Henry's second wife, the bar was approximately 17 to 20 feet long with a wooden handrail, brass footrest, and a large ornamental back bar that displayed all the liquor bottles and glasses. This bar was taken out and put into the barn by the second owner.

There is a rumor of the bar being destroyed in a barn fire, but many stories claim that the bar has moved from town to town in New Mexico. Reports have it in places such as Taos, Red River, Las Cruces, and Vaughn, New Mexico. At the time of this book, its

St. James wooden bar circa 1906 (Courtesy Lambert Family)

true whereabouts are unknown.

In past documents, it was reported that the St. James Hotel had approximately 24-28 sleeping rooms. If we take the 1880 account of the Cimarron News & Press description of the interior of the hotel which states: "4 suites and 5 single sleeping rooms on the first floor and 4 suites and 11 sleeping rooms on the second floor." This would add up to 24 sleeping rooms. Could there have been more? We just don't know, as the hotel has been remodeled several times over the years to add bathrooms, electrical and plumbing, and to repurpose rooms and other spaces.

Underneath today's dining area and bar (what used to be the saloon), there is a basement with a boiler still in it. This boiler was installed in the 1930s by the second owner, F.W. Heagler. It is unknown exactly what type of heating or boiler equipment was under the hotel originally, but it did operate by coal, which is evident by the old coal chutes. There was another boiler in the last room on the south side of the east wing on the first floor. The coal chute for the saloon boiler is now under the wooden walkway by the original front door. The coal chute for the second boiler can still be seen on the outside of the east wall on the east wing, south of the hall window.

An interesting legend has it that prostitutes had a secret entrance to the second floor to service their gentleman friends. Upon inspection of the last room, #20, on the south side of the east wing, second floor, there is a closet type structure just to the left as you walk into the room. It is rumored that this closet housed a stairway from the boiler room below it. This boiler room was also the only room in the east wing that had an outside entrance in that time period. The soiled doves would enter through the boiler room entrance and take the stairs, or ladder, to the second floor to engage in the evening activities…and no one would be the wiser.

Today in the lobby/parlor there is a large crystal chandelier that once hung in the Lucien Maxwell mansion. Also, in the dining area, there is an oval table that was also originally in the Maxwell mansion located on the lot across the street on the north side of the St. James. Each is quite a piece of history in its own right.

Henry and his family lived on the second floor in the area above the bar and kitchen. Their space included a private dining room and four bedrooms. The children were raised in the hotel and it became part of their life. As they got older, they would help in various capacities around the hotel from taking care of the stables and tending bar to eventually managing the business.

Henry opened the hotel in 1881 with limited use, but construction continued until 1882 when the hotel was completed. In a December 1881 issue of the Raton Guard newspaper, it said "Lambert incorporated the original bar and billiard parlor into the edifice, thus preserving for future generations the room that saw the frontier blossom. Built at a cost of $17,000 and is one of the finest hotels in the territory." Henry finally had his grand hotel which would continue to serve the western frontier and its personalities for years to come.

Pictorial History of the Hotel

The following collection of pictures are of the St. James Hotel throughout its history. An attempt has been made to lay out the pictures in chronological order. Some of these pictures have no information behind them and dating is done through elements within the pictures such as landmarks, period objects, car models, tree height, etc. Others are validated by the photographer or source.

This is the oldest picture of the St. James Hotel available at the current time, circa 1885. This was taken looking toward the northeast. Notice the small size of the trees, as if recently planted. There is also a horse tied to a hitching post out front. The hothouse is the one-story structure with the slanted roof under the single window of the hotel. The building to the left and behind the St. James is the servant quarters section of the west side of the Maxwell Mansion which looks in very good condition. (Courtesy of the St. James Hotel)

This is an interesting photo showing the north face of the hotel. Notice the shutters on the hotel and the faux stone block look in the stucco. This is the only known photo of the hotel with this appearance. The trees have become larger and reach the upper floor windows. It also shows the Lambert family. Mary Elizabeth (sitting) with the children and Henry leaning in the doorway with an apron on. Johnnie Lambert is standing next to his mother. Johnnie died in 1892, so this would circa that timeframe. (Courtesy Arthur Johnson Memorial Library Raton)

These two photos are taken at approximately the same time, somewhere around the turn of the century (1905-1910). In both photos the hotel looks in very good condition with new stucco and shows a wooden balcony that has been added to the structure. The upper photo shows a horse tied to a hitching post in the front of the hotel along with someone being pushed in a wheelchair. The trees are now above the second story in height and a flagpole has been added to the roof. (Courtesy Audrey Alpers Collection)

Circa 1910 -1918 with a Ford Model T parked in front by the hitching post. Above the doorway on the balcony are the letters "M.L. 1880." It is rumored this meant Monsieur Lambert. Notice the addition of the electric porch light and mature trees. (Courtesy Lambert Family)

Circa 1915 - 1920. The clashing of two worlds. A horse drawn buggy by an Oldsmobile touring car in front of the hotel. The St. James Hotel sign is an addition. Above it is the "M.L. 1880." (Courtesy Library of Congress)

The St. James Hotel in winter with the ruins of the Maxwell Mansion in the foreground showing the old servants quarter section. (Courtesy St. James Hotel)

Circa 1928-30. The St. James Hotel begins to show signs of disrepair. The paint is almost completely off the porch and signs. The balcony is missing slats. Notice the addition of another "Hotel" sign and an additional sign stating, "American Owned and Operated." (Courtesy Lambert Family)

Circa 1930. This may be one of the last pictures of the St. James Hotel in ownership of the Lambert family before sale to the second owner. The "St. James Hotel" sign and "M.L. 1880" are still under the balcony, but the balcony is missing a section and in disrepair. (by H. Sage Goodwin, Courtesy Palace of the Governors Photo Archives (NMHM/DCA), Neg. #119493)

Circa 1936. Now the Don Diego Hotel and under ownership of F.W Haegler. The balcony has been taken down. Notice the old balcony support pole foundations are still in place with flowerpots on them in this photo and the one below. Also, the portico has been added which is today's main entrance. (Library of Congress)

Circa 1938. Don Diego Hotel. (Courtesy HJG/Frashers Fotos Collection, Pomona Library, CA)

Circa 1938. Don Diego Hotel. Looking at the south face of the hotel. (Courtesy HJG/Frashers Fotos Collection, Pomona Library, CA)

Circa 1940s. Looking at the north face of the hotel. Notice old balcony foundations are missing. (Courtesy Arthur Johnson Memorial Library, Raton, N.M.)

Circa 1970s. The Don Diego Hotel is still operational, but only in the modern annex rooms on the south side of the property, which are still active today. In the 1970s the owner made the original hotel section into a museum as shown in this picture (vertical "Museum" sign). Rooms were decorated in the period furnishings. (Courtesy Arthur Johnson Memorial Library, Raton, N.M.)

Circa 1985. Given back its original name, "The St. James Hotel," by new owner Ed Sitzberger. Ed brings the grand old house back to her glory. (Courtesy Ed Sitzberger)

Circa 2017. The St. James Hotel continues to service customers just like Henry Lambert did in 1871. (Author's collection)

Part 4: The Guests of the St. James Hotel

The Register

The St. James Hotel had two guest sign-in registers. One from 1872 to 1880 and one from 1880 forward. Unfortunately, the original register from 1872 to 1880 has been lost. The good news is Henry's son, Fred Lambert, had the foresight to copy down names on the registers from 1872 to 1885. Fred spent many hours writing these names down and typing them from the old registers. He even went as far as to put them in alphabetical order. Unfortunately, this is not believed to be the complete list of names. Numerous names have been found on Henry's original credit sheets and the 1880s register indicating customers with lodging fees are missing from Fred's list. He also did not include the dates of the lodging with the names. Even though these are missing we still have a wonderful list of Henry's customers that stayed at the St. James Hotel.

On the following pages are a few copies of original 1880s register sheets. Afterwards, are the actual sheets that Fred typed the guest's names on when he copied them from the original registers. These are all on Fred's personal letterhead. Fred has even added an asterisk in front of certain names to identify their importance. Because the print is so small on Fred's sheets, a larger typed copy is provided afterwards with minor spelling correction in the same format.

The likes of Clay Allison, bad boy of Cimarron; W.F. "Buffalo Bill" Cody; Bob Ford, killer of Jesse James; Elfago Baca, New Mexican lawman, lawyer, politician; Zane Grey, western author; Governor Lew Wallace, Governor of New Mexico (it is said he wrote a portion of his novel *Ben Hur* at the St. James Hotel); Coal Oil Jimmy, outlaw; Pawnee Bill of the Buffalo Bill Wild West Show; O.P. McMains of the Colfax County War; James Masterson, legendary lawman; Fredrick Remington, western artist; Mace T. Bowman, Colfax County Sheriff; General Philip

Sheridan, Union Civil War General; Reverend Tolby, assassinated in the Colfax County War; Dave Crowden, said to be a Jesse James alias; John Chisum, famous western rancher; Tom Ketchum, Sam Ketchum, Eliza McGinnis, Bugger Red, and G W. Franks of the Black Jack Ketchum Gang; and many more. They are all here... The register reads like a who's who of Western characters. Both good and bad, it seems they all stayed at the St. James.

There are two names conspicuously missing from Fred Lambert's copying of the St. James Hotel registers...Wyatt Earp and Doc Holliday. So, did they stay at the St. James? The answer is yes, multiple times. Through family stories, records, and historical references, we can place the Earps and Doc Holliday staying at the hotel.

The first time was in 1879 after Wyatt left Dodge City on his way to Tombstone. Wyatt, his family (Mattie, brother James and his wife), and Doc took the mountain route of the Santa Fe Trail which passed directly in front of the St. James Hotel. This is where Wyatt met Henry for the first time and his first wife Mary (Stepp). The second time was in 1885 during the Christmas season when Wyatt and Josephine Earp visited with Henry and Mary Elizabeth (Henry's second wife). Afterwards, Josie and Mary Elizabeth kept in contact by mail regularly. The last time was by Josephine and members of Wyatt's family in the early 1930's after Wyatt's passing. Henry and Mary Elizabeth had also passed by this time and Josie visited with Katie Lambert, Fred's wife.

It was only fitting that Josephine Earp, one who had witnessed the Wild West firsthand visit this grand Old West hotel one last time. It must have been sad for Josie to see the hotel in its rundown condition in the 1930s after visiting the hotel in its heyday of the 1880s. You wonder her memories of Wyatt standing in the St. James Hotel lobby. The Wild West had truly come to an end.

ST. JAMES HOTEL,

HENRY LAMBERT, Prop.

NAME.	RESIDENCE.	Time.	Room.	REMARKS

August 22d 1881

A. Desmonts — Las Vegas

E. H. Wugimann & family. England 24

George Hygart — Providence R. I. 7.30 21

J. H. Schomburg — Staten Island. N.Y. 22

John Alder — Milwaukee 26

Herman Heller — Cimarron

W. S. Vaughn — Cimarron

E. L. McCaffrey — Los Nagio

J. M. Bruntty — Cork

E. Platt Stratton — Long Island U.S.

Tuesday August 23 1881

Thomas Vaughn. Thursday 24 S B

Isidor F. Matta — Cimarron — Bugger

Wednesday August 24 1881

Louis Pinall — Maxwell

Original page from the 1881 register. Notice the first guest is A. Desmonts, the painter that did all the woodwork and murals. (Courtesy Ed Sitzberger)

ST. JAMES HOTEL.

HENRY LAMBERT, Prop.

NAME.	RESIDENCE.	Time.	Room.	REMARKS.
Sunday Jan 15 1882				
Samuel Kelley	Ashcroft Co.			
Thursday Jan 19 1882				
John H Wood	Trenton Ky			
P. B. Smith	New York			
J. B. Lowthian	London			
James Sibley	London England			
Sunday Jan 29th				
W. E. Bruce	Ute Creek			
Ms. A. S. Fuller	Ute Creek			
Jan 31 1882				
	Chicago			S
	New York			S
S Hallenbeck				
Garnish				
Buchanan	Acoto			
N. A. Fenton	City			

Original page from the 1882 register. (Courtesy Ed Sitzberger)

FRED LAMBERT OF THE CIMARRON
SOUTHWEST AUTHOR

P. O. Box 332
CIMARRON, NEW MEXICO
As copied from St. James Hotel Register
Copy -- 1872 to 1885.
Henry Lambert, Cimarron, New Mexico.
By Fred Lambert, N.M.M. Police.

*Clay Allison, Vermejo
William Arkell - Raton
*Ramon Abreau - Rayado
Juses M. Arellano - Springer
Curley Bill - Pecos
John Black - Trinidad
Geo. Blosser
*James Buckley - (Conl Oil Jimmy)
Jesus Abreau

*Crockett, Davy - Tex.
Harry Bull
M. Bushnell - Springer
W. Van Bruggen - Maxwell
Daniel Breen
W. R. Butler - Raton
Bob Bragg
Geo. Buckley - Poier Ranch
Tom Boggs - Ft. Garland
Captian Blackston - E. Town
Chuck-A-Luck Batts - Cimarron
Pete Bedot
*Elfego Bach - Santa Fe
G. N. Blackwell - Raton
Gus Brackett - Verrnyo
D. A. Clouthier - Springer
Mace T. Bowman
Harry Bergman
Chas. Boles
Geo. Buck
Larry Bronson
Matt Crosby
John Chisum
Chip Chapman

A. I. Calhoun - Cim.
W. F. Carver - Diamond Dick
M. C. Crocker
G eo. Crocker - Poinel
Matt Crosby
*T. B. Catron - Santa Fe
George Cassidy
Chip Chapman - Raton
Jim Cayton
M. M. Chase - Chzse Ranch
Dave Crowden - Jesse James - 1879-80
Bob Cowen - Springer
Saudust Charlie
O. A. Curtis
Clarence Chandler - El Paso
L. A. Chandler
H. H, Chandler - Porter Ranch
John Cowley
George Curry
Billie Corbett - Springer
J. E. Codlin - Springer
One-Eye Coreton
Zenis Curtis
Mason Chase
Chas. Cyphers
Coleman
Francis Clutton
A. Clauson
*W. F. Cody - Buffalo Bill
E. C. Crampton - Raton
Chunk Colbert - Trinidad
(Buffalo Bill
(Arrajor Burke
(Annie Oakley

101

FRED LAMBERT OF THE CIMARRON
SOUTHWEST AUTHOR

P. O. Box 332
CIMARRON, NEW MEXICO
Page #2 Copied from St. James Hotel Register
Copy -- 1872 to 1885.
Henry Lambert, Cimarron, New Mexico.
By Fred Lambert, N.M.M. Police.

Dan Dubdir
P. M. Davenport
Stephen Dorsey - Dorsey R.
J. B. Dawson - Vermejo
Bob Deane
Sam Donohue
(Bruce Dawson- Ds Ranch
(Si Dawson
(Manley Dawson
PaTRICK Dugan - E. Town

Jeff England - Poniel
Jim England - "
Hugh Enclsng - "
Stephen B. Elkins - S.F.
J. W. England

John Friel
John Finan
Tom Finan - Chase Ranch
C. M. Forrand
Sob Ford & Dick Liddell
Tim Foley - E. Town
L. Frampton - Hall's Peak
Thomas Fisher
Bob Ford

H. P. Gankins
I. Gregory
Frank Gates
M. Gitskey
Fayette Gillespie - Springer
S. C. Gillespie
Johnny Green
G. Grubbes
Zane Grey
Martin Graney - E. Town

Manes Gallagher - E. Town
Harry Grubbs ---- Miller Old Drill
H. "hugh" Gavin
W. W. Griffin

Thomas Harwood
James K. Hunt - Cimarron
Ive Hatfield
James Harris - Cimmaron
Meyers & Hankins
Mathie Heck - Cimarroncito
Billie Holmes - Springer
Albert Harmon - Springer
John Hixenbaugh
Abe Hixenbauch
French Henry - Baldy
June A. Hunt
Joe Holbrook
Joh n Holland - Rayado
John Hendelong
Jake Hammond - E. Town
Wall W. Henderson - E. Town
Gov. O. A. Hadley
Gus Hefron

Charles Elfeld - Raton
*Robert Ingersoll
A. G. Irvine - I. Agent
John Jacquot - Springer

Crying Jones = E. Town - Freighter
Coal-Oil Jimmy
R. H. Joyce
Jesse James - 1879

Dr. Kohlhousen - Raton
Thomas Knott
Bill Kechner - Raton

FRED LAMBERT OF THE CIMARRON
SOUTHWEST AUTHOR

P. O. Box 332
CIMARRON, NEW MEXICO
Page #3 Copied from St. James Hotel Register
Copy — 1872 to 1885
Henry Lambert, Cimarraon, New Mex.
By Fred Lambert, N.M.M. Police.

William Kroenig — E. Town
Peter Kinsinger

Marion Littrell — Springer
Dr. Ludlum — Cimarron
Dr. Longwell — Cimarron
*MaJOR Lillie — Pawnee Bill
E. W. Lacy
Pat Lyons — Raton
Jimmy Lynch — E. Town
Joe Lawery — E. Town
Jim Livingston — Poniel Park
Dick Liddel
Ben Lilly
Pomeroy Laughin
Judge Wm. D. Lee
William Low
Robert Lee

Alf McCready — California Joe
* P. McKnight
* John McCullock
*Major McGruder
* Joe McCurdy
* Tom McBride — Chase Ranch
*O. P. McMains
*Tim McCallister
*Matt McCallister

Colonel Morley
*Jas.H. Masterson
John Morgan
E. R. Manning — Maxwell Farm
Richard Morton
A. F. Middaugh
F. M. W. Mills
V. Marciel — Frenchy
Dick Miller
George Milner — Cimarron

Taylor Naudling
Russell Marcy — Santa Fe
Herman Mutz — Moreno V.
Lucien B. Maxwell
George Moore — E. Town
John H. Moore
Tom Martin
A. T. Deloche — T. O. Ranch
Chas. Morris

Chas. Nibbletts
O. J. Niles
J. H. Nash

Pat O'Hara
Pony O'Nei l

*Jack Potter — Clayton
Ben Pooler
Alfred Packer
H. M. Porter — Cimarron
George Pritchard — E. Town
H. Pascoe — Springer
Martin Pels
C. Posey — Freighter
Johnny Pearson — E. Town
Jose Paey — Rayado
Fred Phefer
R. E. Perry

Zee V. Russell — Clayton
W. Comp Reed
Mrs. Railey — Utte Creek
Bill Russell — Amarillo
Isaac Rinehart
Fredrick Remington

P. O. Box 332
CIMARRON, NEW MEXICO
Page #4 Copied from St. James Hotel Register
Copy - 1872 to 1885
Henry Lambert, Cimarron, New Mexico
By Fred Lambert, N.M.M. Police.

George Roper
B. H. Robertson (H Brand) MA
Gabe Bailey - Utte Creek
C. F. Remsberg - Raton

Dutch Sweink (Schewink)
C. N. Stewart
Alfred Stone
P. R. Skinner
Bob Stepp - Cimarron
Richard Steele - Springer
Edwin Scudmore
Gen. Phil Sheridan
F. R. Sherwin
T. H. Schomberg
Frank Springer - C. S. Ranch
Chas. Springer
George Spinner - Freighter
James Scully - M. Valley
Dick Simms
Joe Swearinger
Dr. Shuler - Raton
Lon Service - ᵀ Ranch
Prof. Hugh Strivens - Cim.
Jim Sibley
M. M. Salazar - Springer
Bob Samons - Hobbs Peak
John Stewart
Frank Stockton - Raton
A. S. Sever - Springer
W. B. Scott
Tom Schwachhern
D. W. Stevens

Rev. Tolby
B. L. Thomas
Gene Twitty - Raton
Jack Turner
Red River Tom
Lon Taylor
Sam Tipton

Baron Van Zulen
Uncle Billie Vance - Cimararron

W. H. Wilcox
Chas. Walker - Las Vegas
H. H. Werner
Robert White
Tom Wiseman - Raton
Chas. Wimlett
Billie Warner
Harry Wigham
Jack Walters
Ruff Whiteman - Poneil Park
Bill Williams
Whiteford & Davis
Gov. Lew Wallace - S. F.
Edd Wittford
Uncle Dick Wootton - Raton
Ben Williams
Judge Waldron - Ute Creek
Tom Wellington

"In a later register in the in the 90's
The Black Jack Gang stayed almost 2 months
at the St. James.
(Registered under assumed names)
They were:
　　　Elza Lay - McGinnis
　　　Tom Ketchum　　Bugger Red
　　　Sam Ketchum　　G. W. Franks."

Copied from St. James Hotel Register – 1872 to 1885 By Fred Lambert

*Clay Allison, Vermejo
William Arkell – Raton
*Ramon Abreau – Rayado
Juses M. Arellano – Springer
Curley Bill – Pecos
John Black – Trinidad
Geo. Blosser
*James Buckley – (Coal Oil Jimmy)
Jesus Abreau

*Crockett, Davy – Tex.
Harry Bull
M. Bushnell – Springer
W. Van Bruggen – Maxwell
Daniel Breen
W. R. Butler – Raton
Bob Bragg
Geo. Buckley – Poier Ranch
Tom Boggs – Ft. Garland
Captain Blackston – E. Town
Chuck-A-Luck Betts – Cimarron
Pete Bedot
*Elfego Baca – Santa Fe
G. N. Blackwell – Raton
Gus Brackett – Verrnyo
D. A. Clouthier – Springer
Mace T. Bowman
Harry Bergman
Chas. Boles
Geo. Buck
Larry Bronson
Matt Crosby
John Chisum
Chip Chapman

A. I. Calhoun – Cim.
W. E. Carver – Diamond Dick
M. C. Crocker
Geo. Crocker – Pionel
Matt Crosby
*T. B. Catron – Santa Fe
George Cassidy
Chip Chapman – Raton
Jim Cayton
M. M. Chase – Chase Ranch
Dave Crowden – Jesse James – 1879-80
Bow Cowen – Springer
Sawdust Charlie
O. A. Curtis
Clarence Chandler – El Paso
L. A. Chandler
H. H. Chandler – Porter Ranch
John Cowley
George Curry
Billie Corbett – Springer
J. E. Codlin – Springer
One-Eye Coreton
Zenis Curtis
Mason Chase
Chas. Cyphers
  Coleman
Francis Clutton
A. Clauson
*W. F. Cody – Buffalo Bill
E. C. Crampton – Raton
Chunk Colbert- Trinidad
(Buffalo Bill
(Arrajor Burke
(Annie Oakley

Dan Dubdir

P. M. Davenport

Stephen Dorsey – Dorsey R.

J. B. Dawson – Vermejo

Bob Deane

Sam Donohue

(Bruce Dawson- Ds Ranch

(Si Dawson

(Manley Dawson

Patrick Dugan – E. Town

Jeff England – Poniel

Jim England – "

Hugh England – "

Stephen B. Elkins – S.F.

J. W. England

John Friel

John Finan

Tom Finan – Chase Ranch

F. M. Forrand

*Bob Ford & Dick Liddell

Tim Foley – E. Town

L. Frampton – Hall's Peak

Thomas Fisher

*Bob Ford

H. P. Gankins

I. Gregory

Frank gates

M. Gitskey

Fayette Gillespie – Springer

S. C. Gillespie

Johnny Green

G. Grubbes

*Zane Grey

Martin Graney – E. Town

Manes Gallagher – E. Town

Harry Grubbs --- Miller Old Drill

H. "Hugh" Gavin

W. W. Griffin

Thomas Harwood

James K. Hunt – Cimarron

Ive Hatfield

James Harris – Cimarron

Meyers & Hankins

Mathie Heck – Cimmarroncito

Billie Homes – Springer

Albert Harmon – Springer

John Hixenbaugh

Abe Hixenbauch

French Henry – Baldy

June A. Hunt

*Joe Holbrook

John Holland – Rayado

John Hendelong

Jake Hammond – E. Town

Wall W. Henderson – E. Town

Gov. O. A. Hadley

*Gus Hefron

Charles Elfeld – Raton

*Robert Ingersoll

A. G. Irvine – I. Agent

John Jacquot – Springer

Crying Jones = E. Town Freighter

*Coal-Oil Jimmy

R. H. Joyce

*Jesse James – 1879

Dr. Kohlousen – Raton

Thomas Knott

Bill Kechner – Raton

William Kroenig – E. Town
Peter Kinsinger

Marion Litterell – Springer
Dr. Ludlum – Cimarron
Dr. Longwell – Cimarron
*Major Lillie – Pawnee Bill
E. W. Lacy
Pat Lyons – Raton
Jimmy Lawery
Jim Livingston – Poniel Park
*Dick Liddil
*Ben Lilly
*Pomeroy Laughin
Judge Wm. D. Lee
William Low
Robert Lee

Alf McCready – California Joe
*P. McKnight
*John McCullock
*Major McGruder
*Joe McCurdy
*Tom McBride – Chase Ranch
*O. P. McMains
*Tim McCallister
*Matt McCallister

Colonel Morley
*Jas.H. Masterson
John Morgan
E. R. Manning – Maxwell Farm
Richard Morton
A. F. Middaugh
F. M. W. Mills
V. Marciel – Frenchy
Dick Miller
George Milner – Cimarron

Taylor Naudling
Russell March – Santa Fe
Herman Mutz – Moreno V.
*Lucien B. Maxwell
George Moore – E. Town
John H. Moore
Tom Martin
A. T. Meloche – T. O. Ranch
Chas. Morris

Chas. Nibbletts
O. J. Niles
J. H. Nash

Pat O'Hare
Pony O'Neil l

*Jack Potter – Clayton
Ben pooler
Alfred Packer
H. M. Porter – Cimarron
George Pritchard – E. Town
H. Pascoe – Springer
Martin Pels
C. Posey – Freighter
Johnny Pearson – E. Town
Jose Paey – Rayado
Fred Phefer
R. E. Perry

Zee V. Russell – Clayton
W. Comp Reed
Mrs. Railey – Utte Creek
Bill Rinehart
Isaac Rinehart
*Fredrick Remington

George Roper
B. H. Robertson (H Brand) MA
Gabe Railey – Utte Creek
C. F. Remsberg – Raton

Dutch Sweink (Schewink)
C. N. Stewart
Alfred Stone
P. R. Skinner
Bob Stepp – Cimarron
Richard Steele – Springer
Edwin Scudmore
*Gen. Phil Sheridan
F. R. Sherwin
T. H. Schomberg
*Frank Springer – C. S. Ranch
*Chas. Springer
George Spinner – Freighter
James Scully – M. Valley
Dick Simms
Joe Swearinger
Dr. Shuler – Raton
Lon Service – T Ranch
Prof. Hugh Strivens – Cim.
Jim Sibley
M. M. Salazar – Springer
W. B. Scott
Tom Schwachhern
D. W. Stevens

* Rev. Tolby
B. L. Thomas
Gene Twitty – Raton
Jack Turner
Red River Tom
Lon Taylor
Sam Tipton

Baron Van Zulen
Uncle Billie Vance – Cimarron

W. H. Wilcox
Chas. Walker – Las Vegas
H. H. Werner
Robert White
Tom Wiseman – Raton
Chas. Wiblett
Billie Warner
Harry Wigham
Jack Walters
Ruff Whiteman – Poneil Park
Bill Williams
Whiteford & Davis
*Gov. Lew Wallace – S. F.
Edd Wittford
Uncle Dick Wootton – Raton
Ben Williams
Judge Waldron – Ute Creek
Tom Wallington

"In a later register in the 90s The Black Jack Gang stayed almost 2 months at the St. James. (registered under assumed names) They were:
Elza Lay – McGinnis
*Tom Ketchum   Bugger Red
*Sam Ketchum   G. W. Franks"

Henry's Records

Henry kept good records, which is probably why he was such a good proprietor. He left behind dozens and dozens of pages of his credit sheets on different customers, mostly locals that had a tab at the saloon. These credit sheets are not just for the customary number of drinks owed for, but cigars, candy, food, and other odds and ends. Sometimes Henry even added personal comments on the customers, which may have been a tad unflattering at times. The following are copies of Henry's credit sheets on some of his customers. It gives a wonderful insight into the day and the lives of these people.

<u>Some of the Costs at Henry's Hotel & Saloon in 1880</u>

Room: $0.75 to $3.00 per night

Room & Meals Per Day: $7.00

Bottle of Whisky: $2.00

Bottle of Beer: $0.50

Drink: $0.65 to $0.75

Bottle of Wine: $2.50

Cigar: $0.25 to $0.75

Tobacco: $0.20 to $0.80

Cigar & Pool: $1.25

Drink, Beer, & Tobacco: $0.90

1871   M L G & R W Co

Dec 12 ... ... 2.75
13 ... ... 2.10
" 8.75
25 ... ... 3.75
26 ... ... 6.75

24.00
" 31 ... 121.35   1872
" " ... 48.32   Jan 22 By Draft   193.67
193.67   193.67

1872
Jan   To Board by ...
   Mrs Montgomery   7.50   Feb 22 By Cash   78.80

Feb 3 To Map ... .50
" ... Powder .75
" Mustard .50
6 ... 10 ... .75
1 ... ... .75
11 Eggs ... 1.00
14 Salt ... Eggs 1.35
21 " Bread
22 ... Butter ... 31.80
25 " Oysters ... 1.00
27 " Bill by Morley ... 47.00
29 " ... Board 41.42
" Bread .50
" Bread .30
" ... .50
85.12   Mch 11 By Cash   85.12
" Morley's Bill

March 3 To Board
4 " Bread .15

1871 Credit sheet for the Maxwell Land Grant & Railway Company—MLG& RW Co. (Courtesy Ed Sitzberger)

Credit sheet for T. J. Wright in 1881. Notice on row 15 the "bottle of whiskey" is $2.00. T. J. is a reported spirit in the hotel. (Courtesy Ed Sitzberger)

Part 5: After Henry

Time Moves On: The Don Diego Hotel

Time moves on and the Old West slowly fades into a new century. The rough and tumble days of Lambert's Saloon become a distant memory. Schools, churches, and even an opera house are built as the town becomes more civilized. The railroad finally comes to town and business prospers. New Mexico becomes a state in 1912. Life settles down for the wild and wooly Cimarron.

Henry passes away in 1913 due to illness. Mary Elizabeth continues to run the hotel with her sons until her death in 1926. At one time, Mary entertained the idea to make the hotel into a tuberculosis sanitarium, but with World War I that idea was dropped. Frank is the first to move away prior to 1910, where he was working in Oregon according to the 1910 census. William and Gene moved to California in the early 1920s. Fred returns to Cimarron from living in Kansas City to run the St. James Hotel in the mid-1920s until his mother's death. He then continues to run the hotel until it is sold. Fred is the last Lambert to operate the hotel.

The hotel is open part time until it is sold in 1932. The new owner, F.W. "Will" Haegler, renames the hotel the "Don Diego Hotel." At the time, "Don Diego" was very loosely translated to "St. James," although I have a feeling that Spanish language scholars may have more to say on this. The hotel had approximately 25 rooms at this time. Haegler rented out 16 rooms and used the rest for his family and hotel employees.

The St. James/Don Diego Hotel goes through a series of transformations. Haegler immediately takes out the big wooden bar and puts it in a barn out back to make the saloon into a dining room. He does this to get away from the hotel's reputation as a "wild saloon" and concentrates more on the hotel and restaurant business. At this time, it is believed renovation was done to update the building with more modern amenities such as a better electrical layout and the addition of more bathrooms. Six bedrooms were given private baths during the modernization. More bathrooms were added in years to follow. During the renovation, some of the old original furnishings were removed and sold.

Note: Evidence of original features before the updates and renovations is still visible. A good example is inside the bathroom in room 17, or Mary's room. This was once part of another suite before making it into a bathroom. Inside the bathroom is part of a covered-up fireplace. Look behind Mary's fireplace in the bathroom. The same thing can be seen in the Bat Masterson suite by the headboard of the twin bed. You will see an 8-inch extension from the wall continuing at a 90-degree angle. These were once fireplaces.

If you have been in the St. James Hotel you probably have noticed the huge safe just off the parlor made by the "Hall's Safe & Lock Company – Cincinnati & St. Louis." Sometime after buying the hotel, Haegler installs a safe because there is not a bank in town. Where the safe was installed was once a hallway. In doing so, Haegler becomes the unofficial banker of Cimarron for a while, even loaning money to townspeople.

The hotel is sold again in 1946 to W. J. Gourley. Not much is known about this time period, but it is believed that the hotel section stays active and the bar is reopened for business. The hotel changes hands once more in 1958 to Vera Gourley Campanella, W. J. Gourley's daughter. The 12-room annex and swimming pool are added in the 1960s. The pool, however, was filled in and built over in the 1990s. This area became the outdoor patio. The original hotel section is made into a museum. At this time, the owners redecorated some of the original rooms in the opulent style of the hotel's heyday. The annex section was the only part open

The safe that F.W. Haegler installed, making him the unofficial bank of Cimarron. This safe is still in the St. James Hotel today. (Author's collection)

for hotel purposes. The building survived on the restaurant and bar business, along with the hotel annex and museum.

During the museum era, the owner removed the center panels from some room doors and inserted plexiglass, so visitors could look inside the rooms without going in. Today you will notice these doors have plain, natural wooden sheets where the plexiglass once was. The door and door frame around these plain wooden sheets were hand painted to look like fine grained wood in the 1880s.

A New Beginning for the St. James Hotel

In 1985, the hotel was sold once again. This time to Ed Sitzberger, who was born and raised across the alley in Cimarron. The first thing Ed did was give the grand lady back her original name...the St. James Hotel. Ed's family had a very close connection to the town and some of the founding families. Ed's father came to Cimarron from Wisconsin for the health benefits of the dry climate in the early part of the 1900s and knew the Lamberts. Ed's father, also named Ed, was an incredibly talented woodworker, barrel maker, and craftsman. He and his sons did much of the work on the old National Hotel which had been made into a private residence located on the block east of the St James. Ed, the senior, made numerous renovations including a private dining room where the Governor of New Mexico and other dignitaries would be entertained, along with 22 handcrafted wooden doors that are still in the residence. The senior Sitzberger also worked on the Casa del Gavilan, built by Jack Nairn, making handcrafted doors, fireplace mantels, and assembling a wooden cistern for water. The Casa del Gavilan became the headquarters for the UU Bar Ranch and is now a private bed and breakfast.

Ed, the junior, growing up in Cimarron, knew many of the old timers including Fred Lambert, the son of Henry Lambert. Being raised in the town and living in the home behind the St. James, Ed, of course, knew about the hotel and its importance. As a boy, he would play in and around the St. James Hotel with the second owner's daughter, Toni Haegler. After retiring from Los Alamos National Laboratories as a mechanical engineer, he returned to Cimarron. Ed purchased the St. James Hotel not as much as a business, but to restore the dignity of this old established house. Also, to get her back to doing what she does best...being a hotel.

For the next several years he and his wife, Sandy, whose family also owned the old National Hotel as a private residence and the same family Ed senior worked for, would work tirelessly to restore the St. James Hotel to its former grandeur. During this time Ed became very familiar with the hotel from doing repairs and renovations. He eventually would crawl into every nook and corner of the grand hotel. Through the initial renovation, Ed lived in what is known now as the Waite Phillips suite on the second floor of the hotel. While living and working in the hotel many secrets of the St. James were discovered, including the fact that he was not alone.

List of Owners to Present Day

Henry Lambert and Lambert family: 1871 – 1932

Will Haegler: 1932 – 1946

W.J. Gourley: 1946 - 1958

Vera Gourley Campanella: 1958 – 1985

Ed Sitzberger: 1985 – 1993

Greg Champion: 1993 – 2002

A conglomerate of local ranchers: 2002 - 2008

Bob Funk: 2008 – to present

Last Thoughts...

In writing this book and conducting the research I have been overwhelmed by the grit and tenacity our forefathers had during their time. Living in a big, civilized city was one thing in that era, but to go west was another entirely. This meant pressing onward without any idea of what was out there or what to expect. A time where one's courage or desperation to attain a better life was powerful enough to create the drive to travel across an ocean and furthermore, a continent. To endure the quest of traveling westward by wagon on an endless prairie, encountering limited food and water, horrible weather conditions, and attacks by hostiles. Our ancestors were truly a special people.

Today, we would not dream of going on a trip without researching it on the Internet, looking at pictures, and reading reviews. Let's be honest, we get annoyed if a download takes more than 30 seconds or we do not receive our package in the mail within two days. In Henry's time, it took months for commerce to complete the Santa Fe Trail in ox-drawn wagons or by train. Life was tough. There were no highways, trucks, airplanes, outlet malls, or air-conditioning. These pioneers built what they had with their hands and their backs. They built lives out of the dirt with fortitude and resolve. Our hats should be off to these pioneers, for without them blazing the trail, the west would still be wild.

It is said that Henry Lambert was a man of principle and his never-ending work ethic proved just that. In every sense, he was a self-made man. He was also a man of little fear with a taste for adventure. He carved his life out by sheer will and determination. Simply said, Henry's life was extraordinary. A man who sailed the world, fought in the Papal Army, belonged to the crew aboard the first U.S. Naval submarine, cooked for a President and Civil War Generals, crossed the plains, escaped hostiles, met a land baron, and had the opportunity to see and experience the Wild West firsthand.

Henry interacted with some of the most famous characters in Western history, but to him it was normal, a part of everyday life. Through all of this, Henry…was just Henry. A hotel proprietor, who through hard work and a knack for cooking, built something from nothing, raised a family, and left his indelible mark on the west in his own quiet, but spirited manner.

In Henry's possession when he died was a weathered 1830 French book, he most likely brought over with him from France those many years before. It is titled *Vies et Aventures des Voyageur* or loosely translated, "Traveler's Lives and Adventures."

Maybe that says it all…

Kevin

EXTRAS

Recipes

HENRY LAMBERT'S SHERRY PORK TENDERLOIN

Preparation time: 20 minutes

Baking time: 1 hour at 350°

Ingredients:

2-lb. pork tenderloin

1 1/2 cups fresh, toasted breadcrumbs

4 Tbsp. melted butter

2 Tbsp. finely chopped onion

1 tsp. paprika

1 tsp. salt

1 tsp. ground black pepper

2 Tbsp. water

4 medium white onions, each studded with 2 cloves

Butter

Approximately ½ cup heavy cream

Best sherry wine

Mix crumbs, chopped onion, salt, pepper, paprika, melted butter, and water in a small bowl and set aside. Fillet tenderloin so that it flattens out and place the crumb mixture evenly on top of the tenderloin. Now roll it up and tie it with a string.

Butter a baking dish just large enough to accommodate the tenderloin and braise roast on top of the stove to ensure a crusty brown appearance. Place onions next to the tenderloin in the baking dish. Pour 1 inch of the best sherry wine in the baking dish. Cover with foil or lid and place in preheated 350° oven and bake for 1 hour.

Remove from oven and place tenderloin and roasted onions on a platter to "rest" while you make the sauce.

SAUCE

Preparation time: 10 minutes

Boil down the remaining sherry in the baking pan on top of the stove until it is thick and syrupy. Scrape sides of the dish to loosen any bits from the baking. Add the cream and season to taste with salt and pepper.

Remove the string after you have sliced the tenderloin and serve the sauce either on the side or ladle over the pork.

PUREED CARROTS

Preparation time: 15 minutes

Cooking time: 3 minutes in a pressure cooker or about 50 minutes steamed

Ingredients:

1 lb. carrots peeled and cut into four strips in each

One small to medium sized turnip, peeled and cut into eight wedges

Salt and pepper to taste

3 Tbsp. butter

Add carrots and turnip pieces to the pressure cooker and cook 3 minutes under full steam. Mash the carrots and turnip then add salt and pepper, mash in butter.

Do not let the simplicity of this dish fool you. It is a delicious and very different way to serve carrots and the added turnip does something remarkable to the otherwise pedestrian quality of the cooked carrot.

ROASTED POTATOES

Preparation time: 15 minutes

Cooking time: 1 hr. 20 minutes

Ingredients:

4 large baking potatoes

¼ cup oil

Peel and cut each potato into eight lengthwise pieces. Dry with a paper towel. On a cookie sheet, pour vegetable oil and place the potato wedges on it, turning the potatoes so that all sides are coated with oil. Bake at 350°, turning the potatoes frequently so they will brown and crust evenly.

(Recipe courtesy Raton Range and the Raton Museum)

Additional Pictures

Henry's parents, Ro and Mary Lambert. (Courtesy Lambert Family)

UNITED STATES OF AMERICA.

TERRITORY OF NEW MEXICO,
COUNTY OF _Colfax_ ss.

I, _Henry Lambert_

do declare, on oath, that I first arrived in the United States on the _or about 15th_

day of the month of _May_ 1868, and that it is, bona fide, my intention to become

a citizen of the United States, and to renounce and abjure, forever, all allegiance and fidelity to

every foreign Prince, Potentate, State and Sovereignty, whatever, and particularly all allegiance

and fidelity to _The Republic of France_

whose subject I am.

Henry Lambert

Subscribed and sworn to before me, this _23rd_

day of _September_ 1885

R. C. Webb

Clerk District Court.

By _x J. Burkhart_

Deputy Clerk.

Henry's petition for naturalization. (Courtesy Lambert Family)

125

Henry and family after the Big Mask Ball. (Courtesy Lambert Family)

Henry and family on a country picnic. (Courtesy Lambert Family)

Interesting photo of Henry, sons, and a cast of local characters. (Arthur Johnson Memorial Library Raton, NM)

Henry and family. Left to Right: Johnnie, Mary Elizabeth, Frank (front), William (back), Henry and Fred. This is one of the only photos taken of Johnnie before his passing. Circa 1891-92. (Courtesy Lambert Family)

MARY LAMBERT

Mary Elizabeth Lambert, Henry's second wife with Polly the parrot.
(Courtesy Lambert Family)

THREE OLD TIMERS OF THE CIMARRON COUNTRY — OUT IN FRONT OF THE OLD ST. JAMES HOTEL THAT WAS BUILT IN 1872. LEFT TO RIGHT — MRS. MARY E LAMBERT- MRS. FRANK CROCKER AND MOTHER EDWARDS-1908.

(Courtesy Old Aztec Mill Museum)

Mary Elizabeth Davis' Family Portrait

Mary Elizabeth Davis and the Davis family. (Courtesy Lambert Family)

Rendering of Henry and Mary Elizabeth from the book "History of New Mexico" 1891 by Helen Haines. Below: The marriage record of Henry and Mary Elizabeth Davis in 1882.

MARRIAGE LICENSE RECORD.

STATE OF MISSOURI,
County of *Clay* } ss. This license authorizes any Judge, Justice of the Peace, licensed or ordained Preacher of the Gospel or other person authorized under the laws of this State, to solemnize Marriage between *Henry Lambert*
of _____ County of *New Mexico* and State of *New Mexico* who is
above the age of twenty-one years, and *Mary Davis* of _____
in the County of *Clay* and State of *Missouri* who is *above* the age of eighteen years.

Witness my hand as Recorder, with the seal of office hereto affixed at my office in the City of Liberty, the *18* day of
November 188 *2*. *John W. Collins*

By _____ Deputy. _____ Recorder.

STATE OF MISSOURI,
County of *Clay* } ss. This is to certify that the undersigned, a *Minister of the Gospel*
did at _____ in said County, on the *17* day of *November* A. D. 188 *2*, unite
in Marriage the above named persons.

John P. Ryan
a Minister of the Gospel
John W. Collins

Filed this *20* day of *November* A. D. 188 *2*

By _____ Deputy. _____ Recorder.

STATE OF MISSOURI,
County of *Clay* } ss. This license authorizes any Judge, Justice of the Peace, licensed or ordained Preacher of the Gospel or other person authorized under the laws of this State, to solemnize Marriage between *P. C. Bird*
of _____ County of *Clay* and State of *Missouri* who is
above the age of twenty-one years, and *Sevina Valentine* of _____
in the County of *Clay* and State of *Missouri* who is *above* the age of eighteen years.

St. James Hotel

Cimarron, New Mexico

Comfotrable
Heated
Rooms
Good Meals

$2.00 Per Day

Hack Service to Depot

From the 1907 Cimarron News and Press newspaper after the railroad came to Cimarron. (depot service)

ST. JAMES HOTEL

—AND—

RESTAURANT,

Corner of Collison Avenue and Chaves Street,

CIMARRON, N. M.

HENRY LAMBERT, PROPRIETOR.

—o—

THE PROPRIETOR takes this method of informing the **Public** and his numerous **friends** that he is still entering to the wants of all who may favor him with their patronage at the

OLD AND WELL ESTABLISHED HOUSE.

His TABLES are always supplied with EVERY LUXURY of the season, and the Sleeping Apartments are always

NEAT, CLEAN AND AIRY.

Connected with the House is a

FINE BILLIARD ROOM & BAR.

This Department is always supplied with the

BEST OF LIQUORS,

WINES, SEGARS,

ETC., ETC.

Your Patronage is Solicited.

HENRY LAMBERT,

Local newspaper advertisement Henry kept running for years.

1936 picture of a first-floor interior doorway in the hotel. Notice the hand painted murals on the walls and marble topped table. The murals were eventually painted over by later owners. (Courtesy Library of Congress)

1936 picture of interior stairway and wooden railing. The hallway in the background is now closed off. This is where the second owner put the commercial safe that is still there today. (Courtesy Library of Congress)

Former St. James Hotel owner, Ed Sitzberger, in basement under the saloon (dining area). Loads of large stones were brought in by wagon to create the foundation. (Author's collection)

Foundation posts are 12 inches by 12 inches on top of granite stone blocks in the basement under the saloon. (Author's collection)

A door that once held plexiglass (upper part) so customers in the museum era could look into the restored rooms. The lower part of the door and frame were hand painted to look like expensive wood. The plexiglass has been replaced by a sheet of plywood. (Author's collection)

During construction of the addition, doors and door frames were hand painted to look like expensive wood by painter A. Desmonts. This painting is still visible on many of the upper floor doors today, but you must look closely. Original hardware, like this door hinge, is still in use. (Author's collection)

During construction of the addition, suites were added and given marble sinks with hot and cold running water. Quite a luxury in its day. (Author's collection)

This retrofitted chandelier hangs in the hotel lobby, but once hung in the Lucien Maxwell mansion. (Author's collection)

Original coal fireplaces are still in many of the rooms. (Author's collection)

Two original dinner bells. These sat on tables, so customers could ring for service. A previous picture of Henry and family shows one of these on their table. This pair is on display in the Old Aztec Mill Museum. (Author's collection)

Believed to be the original roulette table from Henry's day. (Author's collection)

The original St. James Hotel / Don Diego Hotel buckboard currently owned by Vincent J. Darino of Ft. Worth, TX. (Courtesy of Marcia Redden)

This is looking toward the southwest, showing the town plaza and well, the St. James Hotel with wooden balcony, the west half of the Maxwell mansion, and the Old Aztec Mill. (Courtesy Audrey Alpers collection)

Top: Mountain View Cemetery Cimarron, N.M. entrance. Below: Fred Lambert's, (son of Henry Lambert) headstone next to his parent's plot in Mountain View Cemetery. (Author's collection)

Headstone of William "Willie" Stepp. Willie was the brother of Mary (Stepp) Lambert, Henry's first wife. He is buried in Mountain View Cemetery next to sister Mary (Stepp) Lambert. The bottom states "Loved by young and old alike." (Author's collection)

Left to Right: Original headstone of Reverend Tolby found in the courtyard of the St. James Hotel by owner Ed Sitzberger, being used as a stepping stone. The Reverend Tolby monument that was erected years after his death. The original is on display at the hotel. (Author's collection)

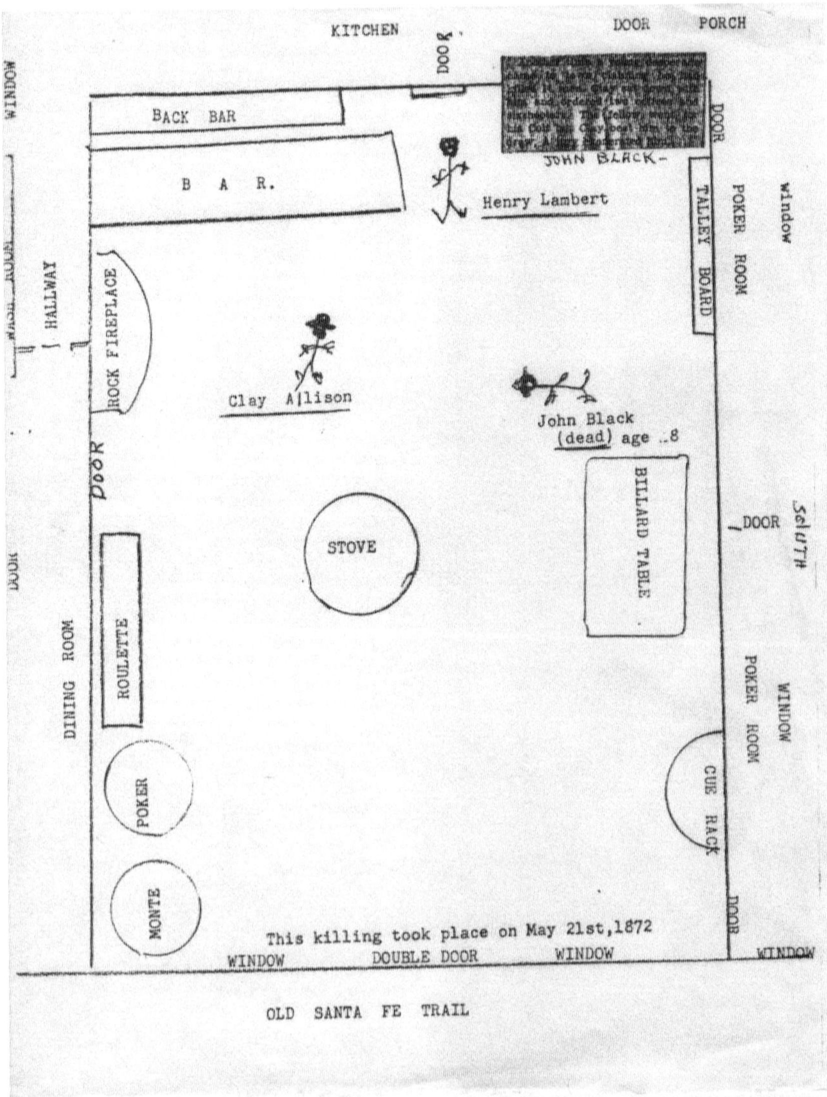
KITCHEN
DOOR
DOOR
PORCH
WINDOW
BACK BAR
B A R.
DOOR
JOHN BLACK-
Henry Lambert
TALLEY BOARD
POKER ROOM
window
HALLWAY
ROCK FIREPLACE
Clay Allison
John Black
(dead) age
BILLARD TABLE
DOOR
STOVE
DOOR
SOUTH
DINING ROOM
ROULETTE
POKER ROOM
WINDOW
POKER
CUE RACK
MONTE
DOOR
This killing took place on May 21st,1872
WINDOW
DOUBLE DOOR
WINDOW
WINDOW
OLD SANTA FE TRAIL

Fred Lambert's sketch of the John Black killing in 1872. (Courtesy University of New Mexico, Zimmerman Library, Center for Southwest Research & Special Collections, Fred Lambert papers)

The remains of Johnnie Lambert's headstone. It has been broken for many years. The other piece could not be found. The picture on the next page is of the historical plaque in front of the St. James Hotel. (Author's collection)

THE SAINT JAMES HOTEL

HAS BEEN PLACED ON THE

NATIONAL REGISTER
OF HISTORIC PLACES

BY THE UNITED STATES
DEPARTMENT OF THE INTERIOR

1872

Bibliography & Resources

A Medal for Mrs. Lincoln Abstract – Emerson
Albuquerque Daily Citizen – Newspaper, 1899
Albuquerque Morning Journal – Newspaper, 1913-1914
Alpers Collection, Cimarron New Mexico
Ancestry.com
Arthur Johnson Memorial Library, Thayla Wright - Raton, New Mexico
Aztec Mill Museum, Cimarron, New Mexico
Badman of the West – George Hendricks, The Naylor Company 1942, '50, '59
Brunswick.pastperfectonline.com/library
Bygone Days of the Old West – Fred Lambert – Sunstone Press
Cimarron News Newspaper, 1870-1874
Cimarron News and Citizen (Cimarron Publishing Company)-Newspaper, 1914
Cimarron News and Press Newspaper, 1875-1877 / 2nd version 1907
Cimarronnm.com
Cityofdust.blogspot.com
Civil war naval salary records (pension index)
Civilwartalk.com
Civilwartraveler.com
Civilwarwiki.com
Colfax County Clerk's Office
    Colfax County Deed book 'A'
    Colfax County Deed book 'B'
    Colfax County Deed book 'C'
    Colfax County Deed book 'D'
    Colfax County Deed book 'E'
    Colfax County Misc book 'A'
    Colfax County Misc book 'B'
    Colfax County Misc book 'C'
    Colfax County Mortgage book 'A'
Colfax County tax journal

Daily Optic Newspaper - Las Vegas, New Mexico – 11/1/1881
Denver Post -Desperado Junction / Linda Castrone 2005
Denver, Colorado - Public Library Main Campus, genealogy and western heritage section
Desert Lawman, The High Sheriffs of New Mexico – Larry Ball, University of New Mexico Press 1992
Desperadoes of New Mexico - F. Stanley, World Press (Denver) 1953
Dictionary of American fighting ships online
Donna McCreary (Mary Lincoln scholar, historical presenter, author of *"Lincoln's table"*-Guild Press of Indiana
en.wikipedia.org
Encyclopedia of Lawmen, Outlaws, and Gunfighters -Leon Claire Metz, Fact on File (NY) 2002
Encyclopedia of Western Lawman & Outlaws – Jay Nash, Da Capo Press 1994
Encyclopediavirginia.org
Findagrave.com
Former owners of the St. James Hotel - Ed and Sandi Sitzberger
Ft. Union and the Frontier Army in the Southwest: A Historic Resource Study Fort Union National Monument Fort Union, New Mexico – Leo E. Oliva 1993, Southwest Cultural Resources Center Professional Papers No. 41, Division of History, National Park Service Santa Fe, New Mexico
Geneologytrails.com
Genealogy.com
History of New Mexico – Anderson / Pacific States Publishing CO (Los Angeles) 1907
History of New Mexico – Helen Haines / New Mexico Historical Publishing Co (New York) 1891
Historynet.com
Images of America, Cimarron and Philmont – Randall MacDonald, Gene Lamm, Sarah MacDonald / 2012 Arcadia Publishing
Kansas City Missouri *"Its history and its people"* 1808 -1908 – Carrie Westlake Whitney / S.J. Clark publishing company 1908
Lady at the O.K. Corral, The True Story of Josephine Marcus Earp – Ann Kirschner / HarperCollins 2013
Lambert family members - Arline Linzinski
Lambert family members – Fred and Rosie Lambert

Lambert family members - Lucille Langeman
Las Vegas Daily Gazette – Newspaper, 1880
Las Vegas Daily Optic – Newspaper, 1899
Las Vegas Gazette – Newspaper, 1876-1899
Legendsofamerica.com
Library of Congress – Washington, D.C.
Maxwell Land Grant: A New Mexico Item - Keleher Third Edition /
University of New Mexico Press
Missouri, Marriage Records, 1805 -2002
Mora County Deed Book
      Mora deed book
National Archives – Denver, CO
National Archives – Washington D.C., Contract books for the
Bureau of Yards and Docks
National Park Service and website
National Rifle Association Whittington Center Museum, Raton New
Mexico – Robbie Roberts Curator
Navyandmarine.org.
New Mexico Commission of Public Records – State Records Center
and Archives, Santa Fe, N.M.
Newmexicohistory.org
New Mexico History Museum / Palace of the Governor Library –
Santa Fe, New Mexico
New Mexico Territorial Census Records, 1885
New Mexico, Territorial Records, 1870 – 1920
Old Aztec Mill Museum, Cimarron, New Mexico
One Half Mile from Heaven...The Cimarron Story – F. Stanley, 1949
/ World Press, Denver
Out in God's Country: A History of Colfax County New Mexico –
Larry Murphy / Springer Publishing Company
Pennsylvania Church and Town Records, 1669 – 1999
Pennsylvania Civil War Muster Cards
Pinterest.com
Pomona Public Library, California, Frashers Fotos Collection
permission by Henry Golas (family representative)
Raton Comet Newspaper – 8/27/1886
Raton Daily Range-Newspaper
Raton Weekly Independent Newspaper – 3/17/1888

Raton Historical Museum – Raton, New Mexico – Kathy McQueary-President, Roger Sanchez – Curator.

Revolvy.com

Rosario Cemetery, Santa Fe, New Mexico

Revolvy.com / Davy Crockett (Outlaw), other information

Santa Fe Daily New Mexican Newspaper - 1/18/1890

Santafetrailresearch.com

Satan's Paradise – Agnes Morley Cleaveland/ Fred Lambert, 1952 Houghton, Mifflin Company

The Grant that Maxwell Bought – F. Stanley, 1952 / World Press Denver

The Mariner Museum and Park, Va. - Tina Gutshall, Conservation Administrator, USS *Monitor*

The Memoirs of Ulysses S. Grant – Weber & Co N. Y. 1885

The Raton Chronicles – F. Stanley, 1948 / World Press, Denver

The Weekly New Mexican Newspaper (1875-77) – Santa Fe

TheWildWest.org

U.S. Internal Revenue Service Tax Assessment Lists 1862-1918

U.S. Naval Enlistment Rendezvous, 1855-1891

United States census records, 1860, 1870, 1880, 1900, 1910

United States Supreme Court-Caselaw.findlaw.com

University of Arizona Library – Special Collections

University of New Mexico, Centennial Library, Map & Geographic Information Center (MAGIC)

University of New Mexico, Zimmerman Library

University of New Mexico, Zimmerman Library, Center for Southwest Research & Special Collections, Fred Lambert papers

University of New Mexico, Zimmerman Library, Center for Southwest Research, & Special Collections, Inventory of the Maxwell Land Grant Company Records, 1872-1966

Virginia Select Marriages 1785-1940

Walkinlincolnsfinalfootsteps.com

White House Historical Society

Wikipedia.org

William Scale, The President's House, 1:409; William H. Crook, "An Eyewitness Account [Part 1]," Rail Splitter 2 (Oct. 1996): 18; Nicolay to Therena Bates, Washington, Dec. 7, 1862, Nicolay Papers; Nicolay to John Hay, Washington, Jan. 29, 1864, Nicolay Papers.

Wyatt Earp's Cow-boy Campaign – Chuck Hornung / McFarland & Company 2016
Wyatt Earp Frontier Marshal – Stuart Lake, 1931 / Houghton Mifflin Company

ABOUT THE AUTHOR

A lifelong admirer of all things Old West and a former New Mexico lawman himself, it seems only natural that Kevin McDevitt author a book on the subject. His passion for research and our western heritage is evident in all of his publications. He resides in the American Southwest.